The Spalaings
of the West

To Patty!

Help keep history alive!

Linda McCormick
5-15-16

The Spaldings of the West

The Henry Harmon Spalding Family:
Where did they go, what did they do?

By Linda McCormick

2015

Cover image – Spalding Mission at Lapwai ca. 1900
*University of Washington Libraries, Special
Collections, AWC1974*

Title page image – Henry Harmon Spalding
*©2015 by Carrie and Allen on Find A Grave. Used
with permission.*

Printed by Createspace, an Amazon.com company

ISBN-13: 9781506025551
ISBN-10: 1506025552

Brownsville, Oregon

Table of Contents

Introduction

My research about the Spalding family began with a simple act of curiosity. In early 2012, I transcribed the minutes of the first 29 years of the Linn County Pioneer Association. That association organized the first Linn County Pioneer Reunion in 1887 in Crawfordsville, Oregon. I was surprised to find that Eliza Spalding Warren had given a speech to the homesteaders at the second reunion in 1888 at the age of 51. Her father, Henry Harmon Spalding the famous missionary, had moved to Brownsville, Oregon in 1849, yet I had not thought about his family and that they possibly lived out their lives here.

So, what do curious minds do? They go in search of the story. It turned into a mystery-driven genealogy study, and it wasn't even of my own family. I shared my new found knowledge in a presentation to the Brownsville Women's Study Club, then at the Brownsville Community Library and again on stage at the 2013 Linn County Pioneer Picnic. By the time I thought I was done, people were asking me to write it down to share with others. I had not intended this to be a project of such magnitude, but here it is. I had to go backwards and retrace my steps in many cases, because I did not document where I found some of the data.

I also wondered, as many other locals have, why the street in Brownsville is spelled Spaulding Ave.

instead of Spalding Ave. It appears that when Rev. Spalding filed his donation land claim, someone else wrote in the information and assumed the spelling was correct. Henry's high school diploma is also misspelled.

I hope you enjoy the story of the Spalding family. It could have been any of our families stories, and I for one, would be proud to have this particular family in my own family tree. Step back in time with me and imagine all the hardships and successes of this truly dynamic family.

Before I go further, I would like to thank a few people who helped me along the way. First of all I want to thank my mentor and favorite author Jane Kirkpatrick. Her inspiration and guidance made all the difference in my completing this book. Because Jane used much of my research for her next book about Eliza Spalding Warren, it kept me motivated to complete this project. Jane also arranged for a coach to help me in the publishing process. I am grateful Roger Hite was there to help and support me in that process. My husband Ray helped in many ways including creating far off stories that would have turned this book into an obviously fictional novel! I leaned heavily on my friends Chris Seale, Gini Bramlett and Laura Holbrook for editing and proofreading. Thank goodness for their honesty and good eyes.

There were times I needed to reach out for help in finding facts that needed to be cited. That was probably the biggest struggle, so I want to thank some of the researchers and volunteers from various museums, research centers and other historical locations. Some of those strangers who helped me are Susan Buce, Eva Guggemos, Sandy Bisset, Mary Mayfield, Steve Lent, Hilary Hines, and Mary Davis. I know there are more out there, and I hope you know I appreciate your help also.

Last, but not least, I want to reach back to my past and thank my high school history teacher, Mr. Jerold Gritz. I can't tell you what he said or did back in 1970, my junior year of high school, but whatever it was it made me curious to learn more about history. This all started with you Mr. Gritz.

Spalding Mission at Lapwai ca. 1900
Courtesy of the University of Washington Libraries,
Special Collections, AWC1974

The Missionaries

The Beginning

On their way to Astoria in 1805, the tired and starving Lewis and Clark Expedition was welcomed and fed by the Nez Perce Indians. They left their horses, cached some of their goods and built five dugout canoes for the trip to the ocean while they were with the friendly Indians. On their way home, Lewis and Clark stayed for almost two months. It is believed this is when the Nez Perce first heard about the "White Man's Book of Heaven".

In 1831, a delegation of Indians made the dangerous trek across the western territories to St. Louis, Missouri, the most western outpost of the

United States at that time, to meet with William Clark. It is believed they wanted Clark to teach them about the Bible. Unfortunately, all but one of the Indian delegation members died before they made it back home.[1]

The lack of a common language made it difficult for the Indians to communicate their desires, but apparently, the Nez Perce message was understood. In 1835, the American Board of Commissioners of Foreign Missions (the Boston-based organization that directed the efforts of Congregational and Presbyterian missionaries in "foreign" lands, including Indian territory) persuaded Dr. Marcus Whitman (born in Rushville, New York in 1802) to prepare to establish a mission in the West.

In March of 1836, Dr. Whitman had convinced the Reverend Henry Harmon Spalding (born in Bath, New York in 1803) to accompany him along with both of their wives. Joining the two couples were William Henry Gray, who was a carpenter, and two young men hired to help drive the livestock to the Oregon Country. The group also included three young Nez Perce who were used as interpreters and laborers. Marcus' and Henry's wives, Narcissa Whitman and Eliza Hart Spalding, were the first white women to travel overland.[2]

[1] "The Nez Perce." *YWAM Native Ministries*. N.p.. Web. 28 Dec 2014. <http://ywamfirstnations.org/indigenous-peoples/the-nez-perce/>.
[2] Tate, Cassandra, *"Whitman-Spalding missionary party arrives at Fort Vancouver on September 12, 1836"*. "Westward Ho" Feb. 2011, *Historylink.org*. Sept. 22, 2013 http://www.historylink.org

William H. Gray described Eliza Hart Spalding:

"She was above the medium height, slender in form with coarse features, dark brown hair, blue eyes, rather dark complexion, coarse voice, of a serious turn of mind, and quick in understanding language. In fact, she was remarkable in acquiring the Nez Perce language...she could paint indifferently in water-colors, and had been taught, while young, all the useful branches of domestic life; could spin, weave, and sew, etc.; could prepare an excellent meal at short notice; was generally sociable, but not forward in conversation with or in attentions to gentlemen... In this particular she was the opposite of Mrs. Whitman...with the native women Mrs. Spalding always appeared easy and cheerful...She was considered by the Indian men as a brave, fearless woman, and was respected and esteemed by all."[1]

Dr. Whitman set up his mission among the Cayuse at Waiilatpu, Indian for Place of the People of the Rye Grass, in what we know today as Washington State. Rev. Spalding set up his mission among the Nez Perce about 100 miles away at Lapwai in today's Idaho. It was located 12 miles from what is now Lewiston, Idaho and near the Lapwai Creek, which connected to the Clearwater River. About a year later another mission was established near

---

[1] Drury, Clifford. *Where Wagons Could Go*, (Nebraska: Bison Books, 1963), Pg 187 (footnote).

Spokane, Washington. That mission was run by Rev. Elkanah Walker and Rev. Cushing Eells.[1]

Early in his work with the Nez Perce, Rev. Spalding became aware of the buffalo's dwindling numbers, and began teaching them how to grow their own food. The Pawnee Indians had to travel from three to 200 miles to find buffalo. Some said the Sioux had to travel 10 to 20 days to find the meat. Spalding planned to teach the Nez Perce to be self-sufficient and to be prepared for the growth of the white population he knew would eventually arrive, by bringing agriculture to them. They planted peas, wheat, barley, corn, potatoes (yes, he brought the first potato crop to Idaho, the Potato Capitol of the World), as well as peach and apple trees. "The true beginning of agriculture and horticulture in Idaho was there at Lapwai." [2] They built both a flour mill and a saw mill to keep the mission working, and raised cattle, sheep and hogs.

While Rev. Spalding was at his mission in Lapwai, Idaho, he had a printing press shipped to him so he could print Bibles and hymn books in the Nez Perce language. It was the first printing press in the Northwest, and is now on display at the Oregon Historical Society in Portland, Oregon. Rev. Spalding's Sunday services were often attended by over 500 Nez Perce, and once in a while, as many

[1] Whitman Mission National Historic Site, *"The Spalding & Whitman MissionsA brief chronology of the Spalding's & Whitman's in the Northwest."* Sept. 22, 2013
<http://www.3rd1000.com/history3/fur/furposts/ww_whitman.htm>
[2] Clifford Merrill Drury, *Henry Harmon Spalding* (Idaho, The Caxton Printers Ltd. 1936) Pg 171

as 2,000 showed up. One of Rev. Spalding's first converts was a Nez Perce named Tuekakas, who came from the Wallowa River area in Oregon. After his baptism, Rev. Spalding gave him the name Joseph. Later, after his newborn son was given the name Joseph, he became known as Old Joseph. Young Joseph became known to American history as Chief Joseph, the Nez Perce chief who attempted to lead his people to freedom after they refused to join the reservation set up by the U.S. government.[1]

For awhile, Rev. Spalding's work with the Nez Perce was met with positive results, but over time, the relationship became strained and his work developed some resistance. Rev. Spalding's personality was known to be dogmatic, intolerant and severe. Some of his teachings were contrary to the Indian's beliefs and customs, yet he did not seem to understand that. For instance, digging and hoeing the earth for the crops was like scarring Mother Earth, also, doing that kind of labor was woman's work, so the male Indians felt degraded. In addition, the Nez Perce thought of themselves as good people and were not happy to think of themselves as sinners. Ultimately, the Nez Perce leaders became disillusioned about how the missionaries were influencing their people to follow Rev. Spalding instead of them and eventually, the Indians created a separation among

---

[1] *"Founding Mother: Eliza Hart Spalding and the Spalding Mission"* Arrival in Lapwai, Women in Idaho History, May 2011, Sept. 22, 2013 <http://womeninidahohistory.wordpress.com/2011/05/02/eliza-hart-spalding/>

themselves. As time went on, the Nez Perce split apart with young Chief Joseph as the leader of the non-Christians, while the Christians continued to follow Rev. Spalding, with Old Timothy as their leader.[1]

Eliza Hart Spalding
1807- 1851

Eliza Hart was born on August 11, 1807, in what is today Berlin, Connecticut. When she was 13 years old the family moved to a farm in Holland Patent, New York. There she learned many skills she would use later in her life, including arts and crafts.

Eliza attended a female academy true to her family tradition. At 19 years of age, because of her deep religious faith, she joined the Presbyterian Church of Holland Patent. When she was about 23, a friend suggested she become a pen pal with a young man at the Franklin Academy in Prattsburg, New York. That man was Henry Harmon Spalding.

When a letter was written to Eliza's parents asking for permission to marry her, Eliza included a message. The letter read:

> *"I trust dear parents, that you will not hesitate to grant the request Mr. Spalding has now made although you have had but a slight personal acquaintance with him. I am*

---

[1]Hendrickson and Laughy, *Clearwater Country*, (Mountain Meadow Press, 1999), pg 176.

happy to inform you that I have found him a kind and affectionate friend, one in whose society I should consider it a high privilege to spend the days of my earthly pilgrimage.

I shall expect that your affectionate minds (in view of what we now anticipate by your consent) will be relieved from many anxious thoughts concerning my welfare. I presume you do not question the object which induced me to break away from your fond embrace and consent to accompany a stranger, to a land of strangers. If I am not deceived respecting the motive which led me to take this step it was to seek those qualifications which are requisite in order to become prepared for usefulness in the service of my Redeeming Lord."[1]

The Spaldings were married on October 13, 1833. While Henry was going to seminary school, he worked at a printing shop, and Eliza opened a boarding house. She later took classes in Greek and Hebrew alongside her husband. Once they decided to become missionaries, they planned to minister to the Osage Indians. At the last minute, Marcus Whitman convinced them to join him and his new wife, Narcissa, in the Northwest.

---

[1] Drury, Clifford Merrill. *Where Wagons Could Go*. University of Nebraska Press, 1963. 175. Print.

Eliza became known as the Founding Mother of Idaho. Leonard J. Arrington wrote in his book *History of Idaho*:

> *"...what Plymouth Rock was to New England, the Spalding Mission was to Idaho." Without the help and work of Eliza Spalding it would not have been the foundation for the creation of Idaho that it was. She changed the history of the West by blazing the trail for women to migrate by land over the Rocky Mountains and helping form the first white settlement in Idaho."*[1]

One of the first things Eliza did was to learn the Nez Perce language so she could communicate better with her students.

> *She could not teach each of the hundreds of Nez Perce who showed up daily, so she set up a system of teaching in which she taught a few Nez Perce a song or lesson until they memorized it. They would then teach it to the other members of the tribe. In addition to teaching languages, she also taught many of the girls to sew and knit. She set up the first loom west of the Rockies and taught the girls to make stockings and "civilized" clothing. Eliza also hand wrote lessons in the Nez Perce language. By*

---

[1] "Founding Mother: Eliza Hart Spalding and the Spalding Mission." History, *Women in Idaho History,* May 2011, Sept. 22, 2013 <http://womeninidahohistory.wordpress.com/2011/05/02/eliza-hart-spalding/>

doing so, Eliza taught many of the Nez Perce how to read and write in their own language. Prior to Eliza's teaching, the Nez Perce had no concept of a written language, since all of their traditions were passed orally.

Eliza's school remained different than many of the other missionary schools in the West. She did not require her pupils to bathe, dress in "white" clothing, or cut their hair. In addition, she taught in both English and the Nez Perce language. This probably made her school more successful, because she did not foster as much animosity amongst her students. However, a language barrier still existed and the lack of an "adequate" written language required Eliza to develop two other ways to teach her pupils. The first was through the use of song. She taught them to sing Protestant hymns and created a hymnal in the Nez Perce language, the first book written in the language. The second teaching method was the use of story and illustrations. Eliza would draw an illustration of a Biblical story and would then teach the story to a member of the tribe who spoke some English. This member would then pass on the story to the rest of the tribe in their language. This strategy worked particularly well because the Nez Perce had an existing tradition of oral history.[1]

Through her work as teacher and missionary to the Nez Perce she developed a positive relationship with them, which was important as Henry often left Eliza alone with three thousand Nez Perce when he traveled to visit the Whitman's. She was often followed around her home by Nez Perce women who wanted to see how the "white woman" cooked, cleaned, dressed, and cared for her children. She was quickly liked by them and respected for her courage and for her attempts to act as a buffer between the Nez Perce and Henry, who was not always as well liked. He was inflexible on gambling, liquor, and polygamy and reproved many people and even went as far as whipping some Nez Perce or having them whip each other. This led to him being ridiculed and denounced by some. Henry was the opposite of Eliza in his relationship with the Nez Perce; where she sought to understand them, he sought for them to understand him. [2]

After the mission's failure [see The Massacre below], Eliza experienced what

---

[1] "Founding Mother: Eliza Hart Spalding and the Spalding Mission." Teaching, *Women in Idaho History*, May 2011, Sept. 22, 2013 <http://womeninidahohistory.wordpress.com/2011/05/02/

[2] *"Founding Mother: Eliza Hart Spalding and the Spalding Mission."* Relationship with the Nez Perces, Women in Idaho History, May 2011, Sept. 22, 2013 <http://womeninidahohistory.wordpress.com/2011/05/02/eliza-hart-spalding/

might be her biggest personal crisis. While she had held strong to her faith through the difficulties of the journey west and the establishment of the mission, its complete failure and the death of the Whitman's left her with guilt and questioning her own faith. She began to doubt whether God's will had been done through her work. Whether she resolved this is unknown. Eliza died in 1851, at the age of forty-four, and on her tombstone Henry wrote a two hundred word description of her, concluding with, "Mrs. Spalding was respected and esteemed by all, and no one had greater or better influence over the Indians."[1]

The Massacre

The influx of white pioneers traveling through and camping in the area brought disease which killed almost half of the Cayuse population. Other political and religious conflicts were also at an all-time high, and the Cayuse became angry and frustrated. Rev. Spalding spent the rest of his life trying to convince others that the Catholic Church was behind the massacre. No clear resolve has been made to that charge.

---

[1] *"Founding Mother: Eliza Hart Spalding and the Spalding Mission."* Leaving Lapwai, Women in Idaho History, May 2011, Sept. 22, 2013 http://womeninidahohistory.wordpress.com/2011/05/02/eliza-hart-spalding/ >

On November 29, 1847, the Cayuse Indians attacked the Whitman Mission in Waiilatpu and savagely killed all of the adult males, including some teenage men, and Narcissa Whitman. Among the 51 hostages, was Rev. Spalding's young daughter, Eliza, who was there to go to school with other white children.

When Rev. Spalding got word of the Whitman Massacre, he mounted his horse and set off to rescue his daughter, Eliza. Learning that the Cayuse were searching for him so they could kill him too, Rev. Spalding changed his direction and went back towards Lapwai. He stopped at the Nez Perce camp looking for his friend Old Timothy, one of the Spalding family's closest Nez Perce allies. Not finding him, he went on to his home only to find some angry Indians plundering it. A friendly Nez Perce Indian found him and took him to another home to keep him safe. Those Indians eventually helped reunite Rev. Spalding with his family.[1] Old Timothy and another Indian were sent to Waiilatpu to rescue little Eliza, but were unable to do so. At least they were able to comfort the children until help arrived. Fort Vancouver sent Peter Skene Ogden to negotiate with the Cayuse for the release of the hostages. He paid a ransom, and a month after the horrible massacre young Eliza and all the other hostages were rescued. Peter Skene Ogden then handed the massacre survivors over to then Governor Abernathy at Oregon City, Oregon.

---

[1] Clifford Merrill Drury, *Henry Harmon Spalding* (Idaho, The Caxton Printers Ltd. 1936) Pg 337-341

The Whitman Massacre marked the end of the American Board mission in the Northwest. Soon after the massacre the mission leaders back east at the Presbyterian headquarters told Rev. Spalding and the missionaries near Spokane, Washington to close up and leave the area. Some of the Nez Perce were glad to see the Spaldings leave, but many were not. The mission at Lapwai was far from the troubles that were found at Waiilatpu, but the leaders back East felt it was too risky to keep them there. Old Timothy was particularly sad to see them go and became the religious leader for the local Indians.[1]

At the time of their departure, the mission had grown from a single log building to a mission with forty-four acres of cultivated land, one hundred and forty-six horses, cows and pigs, and a collection of buildings including: a student dormitory, blacksmith shop, two schools, a meetinghouse, two print-shops, a spinning and weaving shop, a poultry house, a multipurpose building, summer kitchen, a shop, a storeroom, granary, the Spalding's wood house, and a blockhouse. It truly was the first white settlement in Idaho.[2]

---

[1] Clifford Merrill Drury, *Henry Harmon Spalding* (Idaho, The Caxton Printers Ltd. 1936) Pg 352
[2] "Founding Mother: Eliza Hart Spalding and the Spalding Mission." Leaving Lapwai, *Women in Idaho History,* May 2011, Sept. 22, 2013 <http://womeninidahohistory.wordpress.com/2011/05/02/eliza-hart-spalding/>

The Spaldings moved to Oregon City and stayed there for about four weeks.

In the spring of 1848 Henry's best friends, A. T. Smith and J. S. Griffin, drove their ox teams to Oregon City to move Henry and his family to Forest Grove. They lived for a time with the Smith family.[1]

Rev. Elkanah Walker and Rev. Cushing Eells were missionaries from the Spokane Mission. They were also displaced because of the Whitman Massacre and also settled in Forest Grove, Oregon.

Pacific University

All three of the Presbyterian missionaries, Spalding, Walker and Eells were involved with the early beginnings of the Tualatin Academy. The Academy was started in Forest Grove by Tabitha Moffitt Brown, a pioneer emigrant from Massachusetts who immigrated to the Oregon Country over the new Applegate Trail in 1846. After arriving in Oregon, she helped to start an orphanage and school along with Rev. Harvey L. Clark in Forest Grove in 1847 to care for the orphans of the Applegate Trail party.

In July of 1848 George Atkinson, known as the father of Oregon's public school system, arranged a meeting in Clark's log

---

[1] Clifford Merrill Drury, *Henry Harmon Spalding* (Idaho, The Caxton Printers Ltd. 1936) Pg 352

cabin that included, along with Clark, Reverends Henry Spalding, Elkanah Walker, and Lewis Thompson. Besides discussing the prospects for starting an academy, they decided to join forces by forming the Oregon Association of Congregational and New School Presbyterian Ministers, later shortened to the Oregon Association of Churches and Ministers, which held its first annual meeting in Oregon City on September 21 of the same year. Harvey Clark, probably because of his seniority in the region, became the association's president and Atkinson himself became secretary.

It was at this meeting, then, that the newly formed association determined to start an academy, and to locate it at the site of the Orphan Asylum operated by Rev. Clark and Tabitha Brown. Grandma Brown contributed $500 to the project, and Harvey Clark generously deeded 200 acres of land, a gift that went far toward ensuring the success of the enterprise. Clark and Atkinson drafted a charter for the proposed institution, and on September 26, 1849, the group became legally incorporated, an act that represented the first charter ever granted by the civil government of Oregon.[1]

[1]Miranda, G., & Read, R. (2000). *Splendid Audacity: The story of Pacific University*. Forest Grove, OR: Pacific University. Sept. 22, 2013 < http://commons.pacificu.edu/mono/3/#>

It has been said that Eliza Hart Spalding was the first teacher, but that has not been proven. She was likely one of the first teachers. Tualatin Academy began as a high school level school. Evidence obtained from Eva Guggemos, archive librarian at Pacific University, shows that Rev. Spalding sent two of his children there for high school education in later years.

In 1854 college classes were added, and Pacific University became separate from the academy. Tualatin Academy continued alongside the university until it was closed in 1914 at a time when many private high schools disappeared due to the growth of public schools. The first Pacific University commencement occurred in 1863 with Harvey W. Scott as the only graduate. Mr. Scott later became a well known editor of *The Oregonian* newspaper.

Henry Harmon Spalding
©*2014 by Carrie and Allen on Find A Grave.*
Used with permission.

On to Brownsville

After Rev. Spalding and his family arrived in
Forest Grove, word spread that they had come
down from the upper country. Some settlers from
Brownsville traveled to Forest Grove to urge Rev.
Spalding to join them along the Calapooia River
and open the first school. Rev. Spalding visited the
small community and apparently stayed at Kirk's
Ferry, as he signed the guest register there. He
complained that all the best land had been taken.
James Blakely and Hugh L. Brown talked it over
and decided to split their land so the Spalding
family could have good land. In the fall of 1848,
Rev. Spalding took what these men offered plus

more land north, across the river and to the west to include what is now downtown Brownsville.[1]

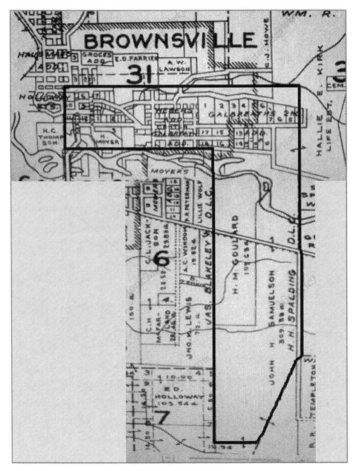

Spalding Donation Land Claim
Courtesy Linda McCormick

A group of settlers including George Armitage, who later settled in Lane County where a park bears his family name, worked on the Spalding

---

[1] Margaret Blakley, Smith. *Interviews by Leslie L. Haskin*, Vol-1. pg 93, Sept. 24. 2013

home and a one room schoolhouse.[1] The schoolhouse became a community center serving as a church on Sundays, and among other things, the first courthouse for Linn County after Oregon became a territory.

In an interview with Margaret Blakely Smith, the school was described as:

> *"...just simply a plain log cabin. It had puncheon, or split-log floors and the benches were simply split logs with pegs set in them for legs. The benches had no backs and there were no desks whatever for us to use."[2] She also added that it had "just two small windows in each side of the building and the door of the house faced west. It was situated on the Spalding claim which is about one mile east of Brownsville."[3]*

Linn County was created in December 1847 and was named for Senator Lewis F. Linn of Missouri, the senator who introduced a bill in Congress to establish Oregon Territory. The boundaries of Linn County then stretched eastward from the Willamette River to the summit of the Rocky Mountains, with its northern edge being the Marion County line, extending south to the California-Nevada border.

---

[1] Carey, Margaret Standish, *Past Times*, Spalding Schoolhouse, August 6, 1981, Sept. 24, 2013
[2] Margaret Blakley, Smith. *Interviews by Leslie L. Haskin*, Vol-1. pg 95, Sept. 24, 2013
[3] Margaret Blakley, Smith. *Interviews by Leslie L. Haskin*, Vol-1. pg 96, Sept. 24, 2013

It was on December 11, 1849 that the officers elected to serve Linn County under the United States territorial government were sworn into office in the modest Spalding schoolhouse overlooking the Calapooia River. Taking office were John McCoy and A. Kirk, judges; Isaac Hutchins, sheriff; N. D. Jack, assessor; John Bateman, treasurer; the Rev. Henry H. Spalding, school commissioner; James Hill, Justice of the Peace; and William McCaw, clerk.

> *Initially, much of the court's time was spent establishing and maintaining county roads and licensing ferries. In addition, the county court had authority to levy taxes, act upon claims, erect county buildings, and license certain businesses. In its judicial capacity, the county court had probate jurisdiction, handled civil actions not exceeding $500, and heard criminal cases where the penalty did not involve imprisonment in the territorial penitentiary.* [1]

The little settlement where the Spaldings, Browns, Blakelys, Templetons, Kirks, and others settled became officially known as Calapooya, or "Kalapooya". Rev. Spalding was appointed the first postmaster on January 8, 1850. He was postmaster

---

[1] Oregon State Archives, "Provisional & Territorial Records, Linn County History & Records" Accessed October 2, 2013, http://arcweb.sos.state.or.us/pages/records/provisionalguide/LinnCounty.html,

until July 14, 1853.[1] On May 18, 1859, the name of the settlement was changed to Brownsville to honor Hugh Leeper Brown.

While Rev. Spalding was at Brownsville, he also organized the Congregational Church, using his schoolhouse on Sundays for services. He served as pastor until he moved away in late 1859.[2]

Eliza Hart Spalding was in feeble health much of the time at the Lapwai Mission. The trip out of the upper Columbia country was a most trying experience, and after her arrival in the Willamette Valley she was never strong again.[3] Eliza died on their claim near Brownsville on January 7, 1851, at 43 years of age. Funeral services were conducted two days later in the little schoolhouse on the Calapooia with Methodist circuit rider John McKinney in charge. Neighbors and friends filled the schoolhouse to capacity. Eliza was the first person buried on the hill that has become the location of the Pioneer Cemetery east of town.[4]

Rev. Spalding felt his children needed the care of a mother and wrote to a friend back east for some advice on a suitable companion. In the fall of 1852, Mrs. J. S. Griffin (the wife of Rev. Spalding's friend in Forest Grove) arranged for her sister to

---

[1] Clifford Merrill Drury, *Henry Harmon Spalding* (Idaho, The Caxton Printers Ltd. 1936) pg 353,
[2] Clifford Merrill Drury, *Henry Harmon Spalding* (Idaho, The Caxton Printers Ltd. 1936) pg 354
[3] Clifford Merrill Drury, *Henry Harmon Spalding* (Idaho, The Caxton Printers Ltd. 1936) pg 359,
[4] Carey, Margaret. "Spalding Schoolhouse." *The Times*, , sec. Past Times, August 6, 1981, October 2, 2013

come to Oregon to meet and marry Rev. Spalding. Rachel Jahonnet Smith was from Boston, Massachusetts and was 43 years old. She was apparently of limited education and people later said she was a large woman with rather coarse features but one who was truly devoted to her husband.[1] They were married on May 15, 1853.

Henry and Rachel Spalding
Courtesy Linn County Historical Museum

[1] Clifford Merrill Drury, *Henry Harmon Spalding* (Idaho, The Caxton Printers Ltd. 1936) pg 369

Margaret Blakely Smith reported in an interview that:

> *"The woman that was sent was entirely inexperienced in housekeeping and very eccentric in many ways. One time she was eating at our house and asked my mother how she made such clear, good coffee. Mother said, 'I put an egg in it to settle it' Later she spoke to Mother again and said that her coffee was not good. After a time we went to the Spalding's for a meal and found out the reason. She put a whole egg, shell and all into the coffee. I once heard my Uncle Hugh L. Brown speaking to Spalding about his second marriage. He asked 'Henry, how did you know that you would like her when she came?' The reply was, 'Hugh, I had to like her.'."*[1]

It was also said that Rachel had never cooked before she married Rev. Spalding.

To help with his finances, Rev. Spalding served as a United States Indian Agent for Oregon from 1850 until 1855. At that time he was discharged as a missionary with the American Board. It was said that Rev. Spalding did not make a very good Indian Agent though. That was partly due to his wife Eliza's illness and death, and then his own illness in the spring of 1851, that kept him confined to bed for a few weeks so that he could not fulfill his

---

[1] Carey, Margaret. "Spalding Schoolhouse." *The Times*, sec. Past Times, August 6, 1981.

duties.[1] In addition, Rev. Spalding and his superior, Dr. Anson Dart, did not see eye to eye, and the resentment between the two became impossible to change. There were issues between the two that were never resolved. In March of 1855, Rev. Spalding was told he would lose his appointment as an Indian Agent at the end of the year.

Rev. Spalding made his home in Brownsville for 10 years, yet he never gave up hope of returning to the Indian country to be with the Nez Perce again. Dr. Dart tried to do everything he could to keep Rev. Spalding from ever going back to his old mission in the upper country as an Indian Agent or a missionary even though there was talk of reopening that area. Even some of Rev. Spalding's fellow missionaries sent correspondence to the American Board suggesting that Spalding was not the right man to send back. The Rev. G. H. Atkinson, who was the pastor of the First Congregational Church in Portland, wrote in his defense, and apparently cleared up a few misconceptions. Rev. Spalding eventually wrote a letter to the Secretary of the American Board, Rev. S. B. Treat, hoping to be allowed back as a missionary. He wrote:

> *"I have ever desired to return, have never felt at home among the whites. They (the Indians) have sent every year for me to return, and have begged to have the mission renewed. This year they sent a trader who*

---

[1] Clifford Merrill Drury, *Henry Harmon Spalding* (Idaho, The Caxton Printers Ltd. 1936) pg 363

has been among them several years to visit me and try to persuade me to return. He...says very many appear to be devout Christians, the Sabbath is observed by the whole nation far more strictly than by any white community...

I hope you will renew the mission. I should advise to send two families to the Nez Perce, one a preacher and the other a physician, man and woman, who have the love of Christ in their heart and consequently will not be frightened at greasy, painted Indians, lice, fleas, grey hair, staying alone, hard work, work, dirty work."[1]

The Board took no immediate action on Rev. Spalding's request. Later Rev. Spalding was able to prove to the American Board why he took certain actions while he was an Indian Agent and was eventually vindicated. He was once again commissioned by the American Home Missionary Society as a missionary in 1857.[2]

The older Henry Spalding grew, the more he thought about his misfortunes, until at times he became morose, and even obsessed with the idea that he was being persecuted. His quick temper often got him

---

[1] Clifford Merrill Drury, *Henry Harmon Spalding* (Idaho, The Caxton Printers Ltd. 1936) pg 371

[2] Clifford Merrill Drury, *Henry Harmon Spalding* (Idaho, The Caxton Printers Ltd. 1936) pg 366-67

*into trouble during these years. Spalding
had no friends who were not involved with
the church and they were either all for him
or else they were against him. Spalding was
that way himself in his relationships with
others.*[1]

Rev. Spalding used his time in Brownsville waiting
to go back to his beloved Nez Perce Indians.

---

[1] Clifford Merrill Drury, *Henry Harmon Spalding* (Idaho, The Caxton
Printers Ltd. 1936) pg 351

Rev. Spalding's Life
After Brownsville

By 1859 settlers were moving back into the upper Columbia country and were staking out claims. When Rev. Spalding and Marcus Whitman first scouted for placement of their missions in 1836, they looked closely at an area today known as Touchet [Too-she], Washington. William H. Gray, who was with them, wrote:

> *"...passed the Touchet, but did not consider its appearance justified, much delay to examine it closely, though the whole bottom was covered with a heavy coat of tall rye grass..."*[1]

Rev. Spalding knew that the area would be perfect for grazing cattle as it had an abundance of tall bunch grass, and it was near the area he knew so well while he was a missionary. He must have shared his thoughts about the Touchet area as a number of families from around Brownsville moved to that location in and around 1859, including his own daughter, Eliza Spalding Warren, and her husband, Andrew. They had cattle and took out a claim on the Touchet River, which was about 15 miles from where the trail to her

---

[1] Gilbert, Frank T., *Historic Sketches of Walla Walla, Whitman, Columbia & Garfield Counties – Washington & Umatilla, Oregon,* Portland, Oregon 1882 Pg 70 http://archive.org/details/historicsketches00gilb

father's old mission in Lapwai crossed on the way to Waiilatpu.[1]

In her book, *Memoirs of the West*, Eliza Spalding Warren recalled when some Indians arrived at her new home in Touchet and all the men were gone to round up the cattle. She was afraid until she realized they were Nez Perce Indians, whom she remembered from the mission at Lapwai. The most important one was Old Timothy. When she told them her father was about to arrive they became very excited and camped out waiting for him to ride in.[2] It is said everyone cried, including the Indians, when they met face to face after all these years.

Rev. Spalding had packed up his two young daughters and moved there in August of 1859. He set up a claim about two and a half miles below the Warren's property with about 100 sheep and cattle. His wife, Rachel, arrived with Rev. Spalding's son about October 20.[3] Rev. Spalding's brother-in-law, Horace Hart settled nearby as well.[4] Rev. Spalding was eager to be back in the vicinity of his beloved Nez Perce Indians.

Rev. Spalding lived for about three years in the Touchet area as a stock rancher and farmer. There

[1] Clifford Merrill Drury, *Henry Harmon Spalding* (Idaho, The Caxton Printers Ltd. 1936) pg 372
[2] Warren, Eliza, *Memoirs of the West*, (Portland, Oregon: Marsh Printing Company, 1916), pg. 33.
[3] Clifford Merrill Drury, *Henry Harmon Spalding* (Idaho, The Caxton Printers Ltd. 1936) pg 373
[4] Clifford Merrill Drury, *Henry Harmon Spalding* (Idaho, The Caxton Printers Ltd. 1936) pg 373

isn't much known about his time in this location. We do know that he was commissioned as a Justice of the Peace for the lower Touchet precinct on April 12, 1862.[1]

Rev. Spalding wrote a letter to a friend explaining that he had already established two preaching locations within three weeks of arriving there. It turned out one of those preaching locations was near Whitman's old mission at Waiilatpu. By that time the U.S. government had taken over the post. Eventually, as the area grew the name was changed to Walla Walla.[2]

In 1860, one of the fellow missionaries who worked with Rev. Spalding, Rev. Cushing Eells, moved back to the area and took possession of the actual mission site that Marcus Whitman had started. Rev. Eells later founded the Whitman Seminary which later became Whitman College. Rev. Spalding was one of the first trustees of the institution, but he was never very active.[3]

The U.S. government had taken over the Lapwai Mission by this time, and Rev. Spalding was trying to convince them to let him take over again as the Indian Agent in charge. The agent the government hired in 1861, Charles Hutchins, did not like Rev. Spalding and did everything he could to keep him

---

[1] Clifford Merrill Drury, *Henry Harmon Spalding* (Idaho, The Caxton Printers Ltd. 1936) pg 374
[2] Clifford Merrill Drury, *Henry Harmon Spalding* (Idaho, The Caxton Printers Ltd. 1936) pg 373
[3] Clifford Merrill Drury, *Henry Harmon Spalding* (Idaho, The Caxton Printers Ltd. 1936) pg 373

away. After Agent Hutchins died in 1862, J. W. Anderson was appointed Indian Agent, and policies began to change. Agent Anderson liked Rev. Spalding and knew how well he worked with the Nez Perce. He also knew the Nez Perce had been asking for Spalding to come back. The Superintendent of Indian Affairs, C. H. Hale, liked the idea of having Rev. Spalding as the teacher and interpreter for the post instead of the Indian Agent, so Spalding moved back to Lapwai in 1863.[1]

In a letter dated February 22, 1865, the agent in charge of Lapwai, J. W. Anderson, wrote to Rev. G. H. Atkinson the following description of Rev. Spalding's return and, in so many words,

> *"...was of the opinion that Spalding had accomplished more good than all the money expended by Government has been able to effect"*:

> *"At the time of his arrival a great part of the tribe was collected at the Agency and I must say they seemed highly delighted at seeing Mr. Spalding again. This was more particularly the case with many of the old Indians who had known Mr. S. when he came amongst them as a missionary many years before. They seemed most pleased at the prospect of having a school started amongst them and also of having a minister*

---

[1] Clifford Merrill Drury, *Henry Harmon Spalding* (Idaho, The Caxton Printers Ltd. 1936) pg 375

who could preach to them in their own language.

Every Sabbath the Indians in great numbers attended Mr. S's preaching & I was greatly astonished at the orderly & dignified deportment of the congregation. Although Mr. S. had been absent from the tribe many years yet they retained all the forms of worship that he had taught them."[1]

By this time others had noticed the effect Rev. Spalding had on the Nez Perce in the past and made reports to those in charge. Letters were sent and reports given as to the fact that around one third of the 3,000 Nez Perce had kept their faith and the Christian practices that Rev. Spalding and Eliza Spalding had taught them before the Whitman Massacre. It turned out the leader of the Christian faction of the tribe was Old Timothy.[2]

The white men who now lived in this area saw firsthand the affection the Indians had for Rev. Spalding. One particular Sunday sermon in 1864, Rev. Spalding had the opportunity to show some distinguished guests in his audience how he worked with his followers. Among those guests were Hon. Caleb Lyon, the second Governor of the Territory of Idaho, Alex Smith, Judge of the First Judicial

[1] Clifford Merrill Drury, *Henry Harmon Spalding* (Idaho, The Caxton Printers Ltd. 1936) pg 376
[2] Clifford Merrill Drury, *Henry Harmon Spalding* (Idaho, The Caxton Printers Ltd. 1936) pg 377

District and many other federal officers. Later Judge Alex Smith wrote:

> *"The scene was deeply solemn and interesting; the breathless silence, the earnest, devout attention of that great Indian congregation (even the small child) to the words of their much loved pastor...the earnest pathetic voice of the native Christians whom Mr. Spalding called upon to pray-all, all, deeply and solemnly impressed that large congregation of white spectators even to tears. It would be better today, a thousand times over, if Government would do away with its policy that is so inefficiently carried out, and only lend its aid to a few such men as Mr. Spalding, whose heart is in the business, who has but one desire, and that to civilize and Christianize the Indians."*[1]

Even though Rev. Spalding was happy back in the Indian country, there were tensions between him and the non-Christian Nez Perce. The Treaty of 1863 required the Indians to give up some of their lands. The non-Christian band, lead by Chief Joseph, refused to sign. The Christian band, lead by Chief Old Timothy, did sign. As a result, the Nez Perce tribes are known as the treaty or non-treaty bands.

---

[1] Clifford Merrill Drury, *Henry Harmon Spalding* (Idaho, The Caxton Printers Ltd. 1936) pg 377

As time went on, leadership again changed at Lapwai, and Rev. Spalding once again became the outcast. There were people there who resented Rev. Spalding and wanted him gone, including Perrin Whitman (Marcus Whitman's nephew). Perrin was away from the mission during the Whitman Massacre and survived. Eventually, Rev. Spalding was forced out of his home and his school. The new Governor of the Idaho Territory, Caleb Lyon, came to his rescue and ordered that Rev. Spalding's home and school be returned to him, among other things. Rev. Spalding remained at Lapwai for another year as conditions worsened.[1]

The Catholic Church was gaining strength in the area, which added to the trouble Rev. Spalding already had with other leaders. The Catholic Church had tried to take over the missionary work since the time when Whitman had his mission. The different churches in those days did not get along in a favorable way.

It is not known for certain what transpired, but eventually in the early fall of 1865, Rev. Spalding, the only Protestant missionary, was dismissed and the school was closed. For the second time Rev. Spalding was forced to leave Lapwai. The first was because of the massacre and the second was because of government officials who seemed aligned against him. As some of his past co-missionaries later said, he worked best alone as he did not cooperate easily with others. Rev. Spalding

---

[1]Clifford Merrill Drury, *Henry Harmon Spalding* (Idaho, The Caxton Printers Ltd. 1936) pg 379-380

took his family and retreated back to Oregon by way of Touchet. There is not much known about this time except that he stayed in Brownsville until 1870.

The government claimed they owned the rights to the Lapwai Mission and that Rev. Spalding abandoned it after the Whitman Massacre. In actuality, Rev. Spalding and the other Protestant missionaries were ordered to leave. To add to Rev. Spalding's frustration, he learned that the Catholics had not been treated the same way and were allowed to stay. Rev. Spalding wrote to a friend about *"...the stupendous mission robbery at Lapwai...by the Government."*[1]

While in Brownsville, Rev. Spalding launched a counter attack upon his new enemies through the public press and from a lecture platform. He tried to explain the wrongs he believed were done to him and the Protestants of the west.[2]

Some of Rev. Spalding's lectures were actually published. Before he left the Lapwai area, he had written some articles for the San Francisco newspaper *Pacific* in mid 1865. He wanted the public to know his stand on how Marcus Whitman saved Oregon and how he had been mistreated more recently by the government. Rev. Spalding had nine lectures printed in the *Walla Walla*

---

[1] Clifford Merrill Drury, *Henry Harmon Spalding* (Idaho, The Caxton Printers Ltd. 1936) pg 384
[2] Clifford Merrill Drury, *Henry Harmon Spalding* (Idaho, The Caxton Printers Ltd. 1936) pg 381-382

Statesman in 1866. It is said that Rev. Spalding's memory had deceived him after all the years and some of his rantings about the massacre were not correct. He continued to write and published a series of lectures in the Albany *States Rights Democrat* in 1866 and 1867. He had written so many that the editor finally asked him to bring the series to a close. Some of his lectures made it all the way back east to his hometown paper in New York, the *Prattsburg Advertiser* in 1869.[1]

A long time friend from Prattsburg wrote to Rev. Spalding and suggested his next move should be to go before Congress. Rev. Spalding had already started a campaign of gathering testimonials about the good he and the Protestants had done with the Indians. On October 27, 1870, Rev. Spalding boarded a boat in Portland, Oregon, for the beginning of his journey back home. He got off the boat in San Francisco, then traveled east by train. We can only imagine what he must have been thinking about how different it was from his trip West in 1836.

Rev. Spalding stopped in Chicago first so he could speak to Rev. S. I. Humphrey, editor of the *Chicago Advance,* who had published an interview he had with Spalding. The plan was for Rev. Spalding to take a copy of the newspaper story with him when he went before Congress. Rev. Spalding also stopped to visit friends in Steuben County,

---

[1] Clifford Merrill Drury, *Henry Harmon Spalding* (Idaho, The Caxton Printers Ltd. 1936) pg 385-387

New York and returned to his home in Prattsburg after being gone for almost 35 years.[1]

Henry Harmon Spalding in later years
Courtesy Linn County Historical Museum

After spending some time in Bath, New York, he was given some fresh and new clothing. There was speculation that he did not appear properly attired to be seen in front of Congress, so his friends took up a donation of clothing.[2]

[1] Clifford Merrill Drury, *Henry Harmon Spalding* (Idaho, The Caxton Printers Ltd. 1936) pg 388
[2] Clifford Merrill Drury, *Henry Harmon Spalding* (Idaho, The Caxton Printers Ltd. 1936) pg 389

On Sunday, December 4, 1870, Rev. Spalding went before the congregation at the First Presbyterian Church in Elmira, New York, and gave a sermon. The response was as if he was a celebrity. He wrote to his wife,

> *"The vast building was jammed full, above and below. I can not give you the faintest idea of the tender care and heartfelt satisfaction with which the multitude lavish their warmest sympathy and future goodwill upon me."*

Rev. Spalding's story was all new and exciting to the people in the audience. He spoke eloquently and kept the people captivated, especially regarding the Whitman Massacre.[1]

Once Rev. Spalding arrived in New York City, he had a meeting with the Hon. Wm. E. Dodge, who at one time, had been the Vice President of the American Board. Dodge had helped pave the way for Rev. Spalding's meeting with the U.S. Senate. Rev. Spalding wrote to his wife about the way he was treated there.

> *"Hon. Wm. E. Dodge of N.Y. Chamber of Commerce took me in his arms with the tenderness of a son, introduced me with enthusiasm to the great number of partners in this great office and then assured me of his warmest support in Washington, sent his*

---

[1] Clifford Merrill Drury, *Henry Harmon Spalding* (Idaho, The Caxton Printers Ltd. 1936) pg 389

chief clerk with me to the steamer, what a crowd in Broadway, he paid for passage to Boston and good bed and supper."[1]

On December 6, Rev. Spalding went to Boston and apparently met up with a niece of Rachel's. On December 9, he met the Rev. S. B. Treat of the American Board with whom he had exchanged letters all these years. While in Boston, Rev. Spalding got word that President Grant had been working on a policy for the American Indians and anticipated designating a religious affiliation to each tribe. He also learned that Grant took the Nez Perce from the grasp of the Catholics and gave them back to the Protestants. To his delight, Rev. Treat asked Rev. Spalding to go back to Lapwai as their Presbyterian missionary. It must have been a wonderful day for Henry Harmon Spalding.[2]

Rev. Spalding went to Newburyport, Massachusetts to find his long lost cousin, whom he had never met. Dr. Samuel Spalding was the pastor of the Congregational Church there, and it is believed that Rev. Spalding preached on Sunday, December 11. Dr. Samuel Spalding was working on the family genealogy and invited Rev. Spalding to spend some time with him collecting information for his first edition of the *"Spalding Memorial"*.[3]

---

[1] Clifford Merrill Drury, *Henry Harmon Spalding* (Idaho, The Caxton Printers Ltd. 1936) pg 389

[2] Clifford Merrill Drury, *Henry Harmon Spalding* (Idaho, The Caxton Printers Ltd. 1936) pg 390

[3] "Spalding Memorial." *Internet Archive*. N.p.. Web. 12 Jan 2015. < http://archive.org/stream/spaldingmemorialcad00spal/spaldingmemorialcad00spal_djvu.txt>.

When Rev. Spalding got back to New York he stopped off at the American Bible Society offices and was able to convince them to print 1,000 copies of his translation of the Book of Mathew in the Nez Perce tongue. Many of those books are still in collections today.

On his way to Washington D.C., on December 22 Rev. Spalding stopped in Philadelphia. It must have been an emotional day when he joined his old school friend, Rev. David Malin, at the Fifteenth Street Presbyterian Church as a guest. In his speech to the congregation, Rev. Spalding shared his story about a "half-breed" boy the Whitman's adopted and named David Malin in honor of his old friend. While there Rev. Malin introduced Rev. Spalding to the railroad magnate, Jay Cooke. Mr. Cooke then entertained Spalding in his mansion and gave him $50.[1]

Arriving in Washington D.C. on January 5, 1871 Rev. Spalding needed to determine how to go about presenting his ideas in front of Congress. Oregon Senator Corbett became his champion in the Senate. In his conversation with Senator Corbett, Rev. Spalding was able to share his thoughts on how things should be changed at Lapwai, including who should and should not be involved. He spoke in front of several committees. Finally, progress was being made. His document, which would go before the Senate, was called "Senate Executive Document No. 37, 41st Congress, 3rd Session" and

---

[1]Clifford Merrill Drury, *Henry Harmon Spalding* (Idaho, The Caxton Printers Ltd. 1936) pg 391

had 81 pages of text. 1,500 copies of the document were printed.[1]

While he worked on the document, Rev. Spalding stayed in Washington many weeks. He later invited his wife to join him, as he had been able to enjoy time with his siblings and cousins in Pennsylvania. He also worked on a manuscript for a book to share the story of the missionaries in the west, but the book was never found. While in Troy, Pennsylvania, he was sent notice that he had been appointed the Superintendent of Instruction at the Lapwai Agency. He also learned his daughter, Amelia, was seriously ill and sent word to his wife to not come east.[2]

Rev. Spalding continued to spread the word of his "Senate Document No. 37", and people loved what they were reading. Rev. Spalding was an extremely happy man during this time. He traveled back to Prattsburg in late April and early May to enjoy more time in his old home. He even gave a sermon at a church that had many playmates from his youth in the congregation. He wrote home about how wonderful it was to be there.

While Rev. Spalding was in Prattsburg, he met up with Henry T. Cowley who had recently graduated from the seminary, and Rev. Spalding helped secure his appointment as a Presbyterian

[1]Clifford Merrill Drury, *Henry Harmon Spalding* (Idaho, The Caxton Printers Ltd. 1936) pg 393
[2] Clifford Merrill Drury, *Henry Harmon Spalding* (Idaho, The Caxton Printers Ltd. 1936) pg 393

missionary to the Nez Perce. Before Rev. Spalding returned, Cowley and his family traveled on to Idaho in August of 1871.[1]

By the time Rev. Spalding was ready to return home, he was a very tired man, having been sick off and on during his trip. He left Chicago on July 3 and arrived in Sacramento on July 8. From there he took a stagecoach to Brownsville, arriving on August 14. Rev. Spalding knew that his daughter, Amelia, was very sick and due to give birth to a child. He stayed with her and her family until the baby was born on September 21, but the baby girl died the next day. Amelia also came close to death during that time and Rev. Spalding waited until she was well again before he left for Lapwai.[2]

Before Rev. Spalding could arrive, Henry T. Cowley opened a school and began preaching in Kamiah [Kam-ee-eye], Idaho. Also, the new Indian Agent at Lapwai, John B. Monteith, was in the process of changing what he thought the requirements for a missionary should be and the methods they should follow regarding the Indians. It was nearly the opposite of what Rev. Spalding had been doing all these years. Monteith wanted the new missionaries to be single (similar to a Catholic priest). The missionary teacher should not learn the native language and instead use interpreters. He also felt strongly that a Bible

---

[1]Clifford Merrill Drury, *Henry Harmon Spalding* (Idaho, The Caxton Printers Ltd. 1936) pg 395
[2] Clifford Merrill Drury, *Henry Harmon Spalding* (Idaho, The Caxton Printers Ltd. 1936) pg 397

printed in the native language would be a waste of money. He cited that it was a Catholic method to keep the word of God from the common people.[1]

By the time Rev. Spalding made his way back to the mission, John B. Monteith had hired Marcus Whitman's nephew, Perrin Whitman, and his wife to be in charge of the boarding and lodging department of the Indian school in Lapwai. Rev. Spalding and Whitman did not see eye to eye on many things so this was a contentious arrangement. They needed a matron for the school and since Rev. Spalding and his wife had not arrived in time, they chose Mrs. Whitman for the task. Monteith chose another couple to become the school's teachers, who happened to be related to John B. Monteith. In addition, Perrin Whitman had been secured to be the interpreter. This meant to Rev. Spalding that, by the time he made it back to Lapwai, all of the people in control were sympathizers of the Catholics, not the Protestants. Rev. Spalding and John B. Monteith received their appointments to Lapwai in January 1871, yet because Spalding was so late in arriving, Monteith had taken charge.[2]

Rev. Spalding made the best of the situation. He found only a few of his Christian friends still alive. His faithful friend, Old Timothy, was one of them. Rev. Spalding started preaching right away and

---

[1] Clifford Merrill Drury, *Henry Harmon Spalding* (Idaho, The Caxton Printers Ltd. 1936) pg 397-398
[2] Clifford Merrill Drury, *Henry Harmon Spalding* (Idaho, The Caxton Printers Ltd. 1936) pg 400-401

great crowds again gathered before him. This time, far more Indians came to him and were baptized. He gave Bible names to many of the converts and to some he gave white people's names, including a couple he named Henry and Eliza Spalding. Another one he named Lorena to honor his first wife's sister.[1]

In the mean time, Henry T. Cowley was busy forming the First Presbyterian Church of Kamiah. As with Rev. Spalding, Cowley had many Indians flocking to his church wanting to be baptized, including Chief Lawyer who became a ruling elder and was involved with the Spalding Mission back in the 1830s and 40s. Later Rev. Spalding traveled to the Yakima Reservation where he converted at least 30 Indians. On the way to the reservation, he was kicked by a mule and fainted. He was carried into a building and revived, but the incident proved to be hard on the 69-year-old.[2]

The troubles in dealing with his superiors never ceased, and in time, Rev. Spalding sent correspondence to the Indian Commissioner explaining his frustration with the situation. It seemed that everyone involved, even at the higher level, were in the same realm of thinking as Monteith. In July of 1872, the government decided to relieve Rev. Spalding of his duties as an Indian

---

[1] Clifford Merrill Drury, *Henry Harmon Spalding* (Idaho, The Caxton Printers Ltd. 1936) pg 403
[2] Clifford Merrill Drury, *Henry Harmon Spalding* (Idaho, The Caxton Printers Ltd. 1936) pg 405

Agent. It was fine with him, as he preferred working for the church as a missionary.

In the fall of 1872, a new person was named Superintendent of Education at Lapwai. Rev. Spalding and Cowley were not satisfied with the way things were going, so Rev. Spalding decided to attend the Presbytery of Oregon meeting held in Albany on November 7, 1872. Spalding reported to his wife that he thought the members there were embarrassed by his presence as they did not expect him. The good news from this meeting was that the Presbytery decided to approve an investigation of Rev. Spalding's complaints. They voted to meet in Lapwai on May 10, 1873. On his way to the meeting in Albany, Rev. Spalding stayed for a few days at Brownsville and found his youngest daughter again very ill. He cared deeply for his daughter Amelia, and it was hard for him to see her so ill.[1]

Once Rev. Spalding arrived back at Lapwai it became clear that he and the new superintendent did not get along, so the church made the decision to move Rev. Spalding to the church in Kamiah. It was a very sad state of affairs for Rev. Spalding as Lapwai was his beloved mission, and his wife, Rachel, needed to stay in Lapwai during the winter of 1872-73, because she was a teacher there. Rev. Spalding wrote in a letter to his wife:

---

[1]Clifford Merrill Drury, *Henry Harmon Spalding* (Idaho, The Caxton Printers Ltd. 1936) pg 406

"May the good Lord forgive the Board &
Monteith & Ainslie [the new superintendent]
for thus robbing me of my field."[1]

In March of 1873, Chief Garry of the Spokane
tribe, contacted Rev. Spalding and asked him to
visit, baptize and marry some of his people. That
summer Rev. Spalding traveled nearly 1,500 miles
on horseback. One day he rode 70 miles! Rev.
Spalding wrote to a friend:

"The labor has been fearfully severe to
ride so much on rough horse in my old age
(70 on the 26th of this month) but my heart
has overflowed with praises to God & Joy in
his wonderful work. A delegation came the
other day again but I could not go, too worn
down."[2]

Rev. Spalding suggested to Henry T. Cowley that
he consider living with the Spokane Indians. This is
where the Rev. Cushing Eells and the Rev. Elkanah
Walker had a mission before the Whitman
Massacre. The work of the Presbyterians there was
quite successful.

The government built a church at Kamiah that was
dedicated in the summer of 1873. Rev. Spalding
carried on with his work there and made the best of
his situation. One time he had become so weak

---

[1]Clifford Merrill Drury, *Henry Harmon Spalding* (Idaho, The Caxton
Printers Ltd. 1936) pg 407
[2] Clifford Merrill Drury, *Henry Harmon Spalding* (Idaho, The Caxton
Printers Ltd. 1936) pg 410

from an illness that the Indians carried him so he could speak to the congregation, only to find that he was too weak to speak. That was indicative of his dedication. He also spent some time translating the Book of Acts into the Nez Perce language. By the time Rev. Spalding had run his course as a missionary and a leader of the church, he had converted over 1,200 Indians.[1]

In November of 1873, Rev. Spalding had a second bad fall while he was cutting wood, which resulted in a broken a rib and other internal injuries.

By April of 1874 the Presbytery of Oregon had decided that because Rev. Spalding had so much success with the Spokane tribe when he visited them, he would be transferred there. Even though Rev. Spalding was 70 years old, and it meant he would be leaving his beloved Nez Perce tribe, he took the position. Before he could make the move though, Rev. Spalding's health caused him to be too weak to travel. He was confined to bed much of the time. Still people came to him to be baptized at his bedside. Even an old Umatilla chief traveled many miles so Rev. Spalding could be the one to baptize him. Rev. Spalding was so weak he had to be held up in his bed to do the task. He named the chief Marcus Whitman.

The last entry in Rev. Henry Spalding's minute book (journal) was explained in Clifford Drury's book this way:

---

[1] Clifford Merrill Drury, *Henry Harmon Spalding* (Idaho, The Caxton Printers Ltd. 1936) pg 407 & 411

...on July 6, when "[Chief] Lot very old came 280 miles" For baptism... several others were received at the time, and with a shaky pen, Spalding wrote "Bless the Lord oh my soul.[1]

Since his accident in November, Rev. Spalding had continued to go downhill physically. His long time friend, Old Timothy, came to see Spalding in Kamiah for the last time in May of 1874. They had been friends since the beginning of the Lapwai Mission. Apparently, Old Timothy had said before he left that Rev. Spalding was his great interpreter. He also said that Rev. Spalding was sent by God to Old Timothy and his people to teach them life and the word of God.[2]

After the Fourth of July, Rev. Spalding's friend, H. T. Cowley, came from Spokane and convinced everyone that Spalding needed to be back in Lapwai where there was better medical help than at Kamiah. It was a 60 mile trip in the back of a wagon on rough terrain. It meant a great deal to Rev. Spalding to be back in Lapwai where he had spent so much of his life. It meant even more that he would die near his Nez Perce friends.

Rev. Spalding's wife Rachel and Miss Sue McBeth (the woman who would take over Spalding's work at Lapwai) were at Rev. Henry Harmon Spalding's

---

[1] [1]Clifford Merrill Drury, *Henry Harmon Spalding* (Idaho, The Caxton Printers Ltd. 1936) pg 415
[2]Clifford Merrill Drury, *Henry Harmon Spalding* (Idaho, The Caxton Printers Ltd. 1936) pg 415

bedside on Monday, August 3, 1874, as he passed away. The details of the funeral are not known, but it is thought that many of Rev. Spalding's followers and friends were there. Rev. Spalding's son apparently was the only child to be present as he lived near the town of Mt. Idaho at the time. A brief review of Rev. Spalding was written in *The Foreign Missionary*:

> *"Although his work has been thus interrupted by long intervals of absence, it is wonderful how much, chiefly by his instrumentality, has been accomplished for this people. From savagehood they have been raised to a good degree of civilization. From knowing nothing of the Gospel, a very large proportion of the tribe have become its professed followers.*
>
> *No man of the Church – perhaps no man living – has, in the last three years, baptized and received into the Church of God so many converts as Father Spalding."*[1]

---

[1] Clifford Merrill Drury, *Henry Harmon Spalding* (Idaho, The Caxton Printers Ltd. 1936) pg 417

The Spalding Children:

Eliza Spalding Warren
Courtesy Carol Warren Harrison

Eliza Spalding Warren
1837 – 1919

Eliza was the oldest daughter of Eliza and Rev. Henry Harmon Spalding and was born on November 15, 1837 at the Lapwai Mission (in what is now Idaho). Eliza has the honor of being the first white female born in the present state of Idaho. Although the Whitmans had a daughter who died as a toddler, Eliza is also considered the first white female to be born in the Oregon Country to live to maturity.

Eliza's early years were in the open country with lots of Nez Perce Indians around her at her father's mission in Lapwai. Because her parents worked closely with the Indians, Eliza thought nothing of playing and working with them. Some of the Indians ended up being important people in her life.

In 1845, when Eliza was eight years old, her father took her and her 6-year-old brother, Henry, on a long horseback ride over the Cascades for business. First they went to Oregon City by way of what we now know as the Barlow Road, and on to Fort Vancouver. Eventually they made their way to Astoria to meet up with William Henry Gray (the man who traveled West with Spalding and Whitman). Eliza did not remember how long the trip took, but it must have been many weeks.[1]

Eliza's parents were concerned that their children might not be getting the full benefit of their education while at Lapwai. Most of the students were Nez Perce, and her mother had to go slower and use different techniques to teach the Indians. They decided to send Eliza and her brother, Henry, to the Whitman Mission where there were other white children.

During the winter of 1846-47 William Geiger taught school at the Whitman Mission. At the end of the session in March, Mr. Geiger sent a message home with Eliza telling her mother what a good student she was. The letter said:

> *"Mrs. E. Spalding. Dear sister, I am about to leave for the lower country, and*

---

[1]Warren, Eliza Spalding. *Memoirs of the West*. Portland, Oregon: Marsh Printing Company, 1916 pg 17

feel it a privilege and pleasure to leave this note in the hands of Eliza to carry to you when she returns home. I feel great satisfaction, and pleasure in her conduct and endeavors to learn, the past winter, and I hope her proficiency may give satisfaction to her beloved parents. She has been studying Arithmetic, Geography, Writing, Reading and Orthography; and has made good proficiency in all for the time. She has also been taught music by Mr. Rogers in connecting with the school. "[1]

In the fall, Rev. Spalding could not make the trip to the Whitman Mission school, so he had Matilda, an Indian woman who assisted Mrs. Spalding in the house, take Eliza on horseback. There is no mention of young Henry going to the school this time. In her book *"Memoirs of the West"* Eliza remarks that:

"The distance from our home to the mission was 120 miles...One beautiful autumn day we started blithely out on Indian ponies, our supplies loaded on a pack horse. We traveled three days and made three camps at night. Each camp was in a lonely place, not a soul near us. We could hear the yelping chorus of the coyotes, and the howling of the big gray wolves. We ate together and shared the same bed, and I remember today, with the respect due this

---

[1] Clifford Merrill Drury, *Henry Harmon Spalding* (Idaho, The Caxton Printers Ltd. 1936) pg 312

sturdy Indian woman, how careful she was to hold the family prayers. She has long since joined her fathers, but Matilda, the faithful, will be remembered with gratitude as long as memory remains with the children of Henry Harmon Spalding."[1]

Eliza had just turned 10 on November 15, when there was tension at the Whitman Mission. She would not have been aware of the problems, but ended up in the middle of them. On November 29, 1847, some of the Cayuse Indians took it upon themselves to attack the mission settlement. They were angry because of the increased presence of white settlers and the number of tribal deaths from white man's diseases, among other issues. Marcus and Narcissa were targeted in particular. Much has been written about the bloody Whitman Massacre and poor Eliza witnessed much of the horror first hand.

Eliza and approximately 50 other women and children were held hostage for almost a month. Only two men survived the massacre. W.D. Canfield was injured but was able to get to Lapwai to warn Mrs. Spalding and the Nez Perce.

The other male survivor was Josiah Osborn. Mr. Osborn, his wife, and children were able to pull up a floor board and hide under the house until nightfall. They were able to escape in the dark of night to Fort Walla Walla, 20 miles away. On a

---

[1] Warren, Eliza Spalding. *Memoirs of the West.* Portland, Oregon: Marsh Printing Company, 1916 pg 16

side note, the Josiah Osborn family had homesteaded in Brownsville in 1845. Marcus Whitman sent word to Josiah that he wanted to hire him to build a grist mill and to do other carpentry work at the mission. The Osborns had only been there a short time before the massacre.

Because she could speak and understand the Nez Perce language, Eliza was used as an interpreter by the Cayuse. Their language must have been similar enough that she could understand and translate for the other hostages.

While the Cayuse kept the hostages, Old Timothy (one of Rev. Spalding's closest Nez Perce friends) went to the Whitman Mission to try and rescue little Eliza. The Cayuse would not release her. That was the first time Eliza cried during the ordeal. Old Timothy wiped her tears with her apron and told her not to worry and that she would see her mother again.[1]

On December 19, 1847, Peter Skene Ogden, from Fort Vancouver, arrived at Fort Walla Walla. He sent word to the leaders of the Cayuse to meet with him there for a council. The council began on December 23. Ogden succeeded in arranging for the freedom of the hostages, and on December 29, the hostages were led away from the site of the massacre to Fort Walla Walla where Eliza and the others waited 3 days for the Spalding family to

---

[1]Warren, Eliza Spalding. *Memoirs of the West*. Portland, Oregon: Marsh Printing Company, 1916 pg 30

arrive. From there they were brought by boat to Oregon City.[1]

Soon after arriving in Oregon City, the family moved to Forest Grove to be near friends and the other missionaries from Spokane.

As noted earlier, Rev. Spalding was offered an opportunity to become the first teacher in Brownsville. He accepted the offer and moved his family once again. Young Eliza had more changes in her life as she settled in to her new home in the Willamette Valley. After the Spalding family came to Brownsville in the spring of 1849, Eliza and her siblings studied at their father's new school.

The trial for the Whitman Massacre attackers was scheduled for the spring of 1850 in Oregon City. The prosecutor, U.S. Attorney Amory Holbrook, summoned young Eliza to testify at the grand jury and possibly in the trial. It is assumed that only Rev. Spalding and young Eliza made the trip and left the rest of the family in Brownsville.

The grand jury convened to indict the five Indians on May 13, 1850. Along with Eliza, there were more than two dozen witnesses summoned to testify, yet only seven actually gave a testimony. Many of the witnesses were held captive as prisoners with her for a month after the massacre.[2]

---

[1] Erwin N. Thompson, *Shallow Grave at Waiilatpu: The Sagers' West*, (Portland, Oregon: Glass-Dahlstrom Printers, 1969) pg 116-119
[2] Lansing, Ronald B. *Juggernaut, the Whitman Massacre Trial*. : Oregon Historical Society, 1993. pg 64

Eliza was only 12 years old when she had to testify before the grand jury. She later recalled that:

> *"I was nearly as frightened in the courtroom as I was while held prisoner. The lawyers asked such questions about the massacre and the Indians looked so threatening that altogether it was a most unpleasant experience."*[1]

Interestingly, only four of the witnesses who gave testimony at the grand jury were called on to testify at the actual trial. Eliza was not one of them. It was speculated that because she grew up with the Nez Perce Indians at the Spalding Mission, and she had been the only hostage who was able to communicate in the Indian language with her captors, she might be too sympathetic to the five Cayuse on trial.

The trial began on May 21, 1850, with the verdict being read on May 24. The five Cayuse Indians were hung in Oregon City on June 3, 1850, in front of a large crowd of onlookers. It is not known if Rev. Spalding and Eliza stayed for this event.

Eliza's mother had been sickly since her trip to the west with the Whitmans. Some have speculated that she had tuberculosis. On January 7, 1851, Eliza Hart Spalding passed away leaving her eldest daughter, Eliza, to take over the responsibility of raising and caring for the family. Three years later,

---

[1] Lansing, Ronald B. *Juggernaut, the Whitman Massacre Trial.* : Oregon Historical Society, 1993. pg 65

Eliza would make her own home with a husband.

Andrew Jackson Warren worked for a cattle rancher in the area, and had not been in the west very long when he met Eliza Spalding. Andrew was older than Eliza so they would not have met at school

At 16, Eliza married Andrew J. Warren on May 11, 1854. Her father did not approve of this marriage as he believed that Andrew was a drunkard. In some interviews by locals of that time, it was said that Rev. Spalding would go about town telling folks his daughter Eliza was dead.[1]

At some point the Warrens bought a ranch on what is known today as Mountain Home Road, complete with a creek running through the property named Warren Creek.

Andrew Jackson Warren
Courtesy Carol Warren Harrison

In the early years, Eliza convinced her sister, Amelia, to come live with them and help her on the ranch. Since Andrew was not available for much of the chores, Eliza and

---

[1]Mrs. Elias, Marsters. Interview by Leslie Haskins. *W.P.A. Works Project* 08 Nov 1937. Nov . Print.

Amelia did most of the transporting of water from the creek or well, collecting firewood and other chores. It is believed that Amelia first hurt her back doing these chores.

Andrew and Eliza's first child was named America Jane Warren, born on November 7, 1856. A little over two years later Martha Elizabeth (Lizzie) was born on January 9, 1859.

In 1859, they moved with another local family to Touchet, Washington, with 300 head of cattle and a team of oxen. Andrew and some others crossed the Cascades with the cattle while the women and children took the oxen to Portland and on to The Dalles where they met the men. Eliza's father followed them to Touchet not long after this. Word was passed around that the bunch grass that grew there was perfect for cattle and the land was fertile for crops. Touchet is west of Walla Walla and not very far from the old Whitman Mission.[1]

Not long after they had settled in, the men left to tend the cattle leaving Eliza and the children alone. Seeing a dust cloud and then recognizing that Indians were approaching, Eliza feared for her and her children's lives. The Indians jumped off their horses and then asked if she was Eliza. One of those Indians was Old Timothy who saved her family after the Whitman Massacre. He had heard she was in the area and was very happy to see her again. They were even more excited to learn that

---

[1] Clifford Merrill Drury, *Henry Harmon Spalding* (Idaho, The Caxton Printers Ltd. 1936) pg 372

her father, Rev. Spalding, was coming so they camped on the property to wait his arrival the next day. Since they had not seen each other in many years, they had much to discuss.

Old Timothy held the Spaldings in high regard, especially Rev. Spalding's wife Eliza. In Eliza Spalding Warren's memoir she wrote:

"They speak of Timothy's conversion under the teaching of my mother. In asking the blessing over his meals, he would end with these words, "In the name of Jesus Christ and Mrs. Spalding." Her memory was very precious to confiding old Timothy."[1]

Rev. Spalding arrived at Touchet on approximately August 18, 1859, with young Martha and Amelia. Rev. Spalding's wife, Rachel and his son, Henry arrived around October 20. Rev. Spalding's ultimate dream was to someday move back to Lapwai to be with his friends.

Rev. Spalding and his family ended up taking a claim about two and a half miles south of the Warren claim. Rev. Spalding's brother-in-law, Horace Hart, had about 100 sheep and cattle and also took a claim nearby.[2]

---

[1] Warren, Eliza Spalding. *Memoirs of the West*. Portland, Oregon: Marsh Printing Company, 1916 pg 35
[2] Clifford Merrill Drury, *Henry Harmon Spalding* (Idaho, The Caxton Printers Ltd. 1936) pg 373

It is not known why, but in 1861, the Warrens sold their cattle and moved back to their ranch in Brownsville. According to Eliza, the winter of 1862 was particularly bad and her father lost almost all of his stock.[1]

Andrew and Eliza welcomed Amelia (Minnie) Warren's birth in 1862, and their only son, James (Jimmy) Henry Warren, was born on August 12, 1866. Both of these children were born in Brownsville.

The Brownsville Woolen Mill had burned in the mid 60s and the community rallied together to fund the rebuilding project. It was found that Andrew bought 200 shares at $100 per share in 1865.

Sometime in 1873, the Warren family moved to a remote area in Central Oregon called Grizzly. It was about 25 miles from Prineville on Willow Creek, and this was where they chose to settle with their cattle. Their young son, James, (he went by the name Jimmy then) had asthma and the dry desert air was better for him.

A couple of years after they arrived in Grizzly, Eliza sent 12-year-old Jimmy along with his dad on a cattle ride. This was during the Indian uprisings in the area. Jimmy had fallen from his horse the day before so the men told him to stay at camp and make some beef jerky at the camp fire. While all alone he noticed Modoc Indians ride up on a hill

---

[1] Warren, Eliza Spalding. *Memoirs of the West*. Portland, Oregon: Marsh Printing Company, 1916 pg 34

and watch him, then leave and come back. That night, when the men got back to camp, they decided that if the Indians returned, they should stay and fight. Little Jimmy was to ride an old race horse named Croppy the 12 miles back to Prineville to get help. They waited a few more days, then decided the Indian threat had died down and it was safe to leave the cattle to graze. Weeks later the Indians did raid the area and all the cattle were captured.[1]

The Warren Family
Courtesy Carol Warren Harrison

Andrew and Eliza's daughter, America Jane, married Joseph Henry Crooks on October 3, 1873 at her parent's home in Brownsville. They settled in at Joe's ranch on Willow Creek, not far from the Warren ranch near Grizzly. Joseph's family was from the Willamette Valley. His father, John Turley Crooks, was a member of the first territorial

[1] Stover, Elsie G. "America Crooks." In *The Pioneer Story*. Prineville: Bend Bulletin, 1950.

legislature.[1] It is assumed that the wedding was held in Brownsville so it was convenient for Joseph's parents.

America and Joseph had six children; John (Warren) Warren, Effie Loretta Crooks Simpson, Minnie Florence Crooks Clifton, Charles Adrian (Adrian) and Adelle Beulah (Beulah) Crooks Bechtell. Later, the family moved into the town of Prineville and was involved in the community there.

America Jane Warren Crooks with
her granddaughter, Dorothy
Courtesy of Diane Herd & Sharla Pitts

[1] "Crook County Genealogical Society Newsletter." April 1, 2007. Accessed August 23, 2014. http://www.bowmanmuseum.org/files/Genealogy.pdf.

Eliza's second daughter, Martha Elizabeth (Lizzie), married James Granville Calloway in August of 1874 in Brownsville. Lizzie had three children, a daughter (unknown name), Maud Calloway Childs and Logan Cecil (there was a ranch hand named Logan Cecil so it is thought he was named for the ranch hand).

Lizzie died at the age of 23 years in 1882. Eliza took care of the children until they were almost grown when James remarried and had three more children.

The 1880 census shows that Eliza was back in Brownsville without Andrew. She had her two youngest children with her, Minnie and James. Eliza's sister, Martha, and three of her children; Minnie, Lee and Eliza were also with her. Interestingly enough, Eliza's daughter, Lizzie, and her husband, James Calloway, lived next door.

A possible explanation for Andrew's absence is he is listed as being in Prineville in the 1880 Wasco County census as a stock raiser. He could have been on a cattle drive to Montana during this time, as many stock raisers did that year.

Amelia (Minnie) Warren married Fred Forrest Illsley on October 5, 1883, in Albany, but they later moved to Sitka, Alaska, and eventually to Seattle. They had one daughter, Cassa Geneva.

Eliza's brother Henry, with his wife and family, lived in Almota, Washington. In 1884 Eliza decided to travel north to see them. While she was there, she took the opportunity to travel a little farther to see her father's old mission site in Lapwai.

Instead of traveling by horseback, as she had done as a child, this time as a 47-year-old she took a steamboat up the Snake River. In her book *"Memoirs of the West"*, Eliza describes seeing her old home for the first time since she was 10 years old:

> *"When we came to the old house and stood at the door we saw an old Indian at the fireplace kindling the fire. He used to live with us a good deal of the time while we lived there. He was deaf and dumb, but was very useful about the place. Soon as he looked up and saw me, in an instant his countenance lit up. He showed all kinds of pleasure to see me. I turned to the man near me and said "Is it possible that he remembers me?" I said, "Ask him if he knows who I am?" and he did with signs. The old Indian, his name was "Mustups," answered back with his signs, "Yes, it is Eliza; I knew it was her as soon as I saw her." He went on then and told how he would rock the cradle for mother when I was a babe, and how he would look after me after I got to running around to keep me from getting in to the water. He said, "These trees are hers, everything here is hers." It was truly affecting to see the poor old mute*

so enthused with pleasure at meeting with me. I told the man to tell him how pleased I was to see him in what was left of the old house and of the many changes since we left there; that my father and mother were both dead; that I had a family all grown up and married, but the youngest, and that the Indians were becoming more and more civilized, and that the country was being settled up by the white people everywhere. [1]

Andrew Warren was in failing health. He died on November 4, 1886, and was buried in Brownsville. Not long after his death their son, James married Nancy Jane (Nannie) Wiseman in Albany, Oregon on February 24, 1887. Eliza was now alone at home. By 1892, James and his family had moved to Central Washington.

James and Nannie Warren had six children with five growing to adulthood. Their children were Berle, Glenn Durelle (died at 7 years old), Verne Douglas, Carl Byron, Reba Junieta, and James A.

The first reunion of the homesteaders living in Linn County was held in Crawfordsville, Oregon, in 1887. The next year Eliza, age 50, was asked to give a speech at the reunion. On the afternoon of June 27, 1888, Eliza stood before the early pioneers of Linn County who had gathered in Crawfordsville for the second reunion and gave this speech:

---

[1] Warren, Eliza Spalding. *Memoirs of the West*. Portland, Oregon: Marsh Printing Company, 1916 pg 36

"I think I will first have to say that this is a very embarrassing position for me to undertake, never having had practice nor experience in speaking, or reading, in public, and but little courage; putting all together making it very embarrassing indeed. Nor do I think that I would have undertaken it now, but I have so often been solicited to say something or write, that I had about made up my mind that if I ever intended to say anything, that it was about time to make a start. I also was impressed with a notice which I saw in the Oregonian a short time ago , that George H. Himes, secretary of the Pioneer Association at Portland had published, in which he says much valuable matter that might have been preserved, is now lost because pioneers have not fully realized their responsibility to those who are to follow, that death has made sad havoc in the ranks during the past year, in a few years there will be none left to tell the story, and the places that now know us will no us no more.

Many of you know no doubt, that I am an old Oregonian. Mr. and Mrs. Spalding were my parents, and in company with Dr. Whitman and wife came to Oregon in 1836, as missionaries to the Indians. My mother and Mrs. Whitman were the first white women that crossed the Rocky Mountains. They were obliged to travel horse back most of the way, and the hardships and dangers that they had to go through was wonderful that they could survive such a trip. My mother's health being very poor most of the time. I was born in Oregon in 1837, it was Oregon Territory and Washington Territory at that time, but since has been divided into Idaho Territory and Washington Territory and State of Oregon, which makes my birth place in Idaho, where the Lapwai Agency is now situated. My father and mother were with the Nez Perce Indians. Dr. Whitman and wife were with the Cayuse Indians, near where the City of Walla Walla is now situated, and one hundred miles from where we lived. They were our nearest neighbor. We lived there till I was ten years old, so you see I had not school advantages. I became quite well acquainted with the ways and customs of the Indians, and could speak their language as well as I could my own. Father and Mother taught them so that many of them could read and write quite well in their own language, and some to card and spin and weave quite nicely. We have witnessed their war dances and their sham dances and other performances. We traveled over the country horse back and pack horses the same as the Indians, and camped where night would overtake us, and crossed the rivers in canoes, and swam our horses. But once we were caught, we attempted to ford the Clear Water river where Lewiston is now situated, and got into swimming water, of course we had to stem it through, it was night and we had ten miles yet to go before we reached home; the weather was cold, and our clothes were soon frozen. It seems to me that there is hardly a day passes but what my memory wanders back to those childhood days and scenes. In the fall there would be some emigrant families that would stop at Dr. Whitman's to spend the winter and rest themselves and their given out teams, and in the spring come on to this valley. Of course there would be enough children to have school through the winter. When I was nine years old my parents sent me over to attend school that winter. Father was so busy he could not take me, and they sent me in the care of an Indian woman, she helped my mother about the house a good deal. We were out three days and two nights alone. I doubt whether there is a mother in this crowd that would risk a child of theirs in that way, but I was perfectly safe in her care. The next winter when I was ten years old my father took me over to attend school again, that is how I came to be there at the time of that massacre, when the Indians murdered Dr. Whitman and wife, and twelve of the emigrant men. That was the first day of school, and about noon that the crash was made. It seems like I can almost hear the hideous war whoops, the firing of guns, the running to and fro. Us poor frightened children huddled up and tried to hide, but they soon found us and brought us out. I felt sure our time had come. I put my apron to my face so that I would not see the guns pointed at us. For some reason they did not murder the women and children, but kept us as captives for three weeks. We were bought and rescued by the Hudson Bay Company, who were commanding at Vancouver at that time. In a few days my mother received word of what had happened to Dr. Whitman's, of course she was frantic, she sent two of our Indians right away to see what had become of father and myself. When they came they thought they would take me right home, but the Indians would not let me go. Timothy was the name of the Indian that came for me. When he told me that they would not take me that the Indians would not let me go, I then for the first time broke down in tears, it seemed as if my heart would burst, Timothy wiped the tears from my face, and said "poor Eliza don't cry you shall see your mother." Father had a very narrow escape in getting back home, he was out six days and nights without anything to eat. We all came down the Columbia River in an open boat in December, and had a severe trip. In 1849 we moved up to this valley near where Brownsville is now situated. In 1851 my mother died and was the first person buried at the cemetery near Brownsville, now number the graves that are there now. Neighbors were scarce and far between, it was nothing to walk three or four miles to visit each other. We lived in small log houses generally one room would consist all, our cooking was done by the fireplace. Visitors would generally stay overnight. That was the way we generally visited then and often take something that we thought our neighbor would not have, something good to eat you know those days, and go for miles to church horseback and with teams. But again we feel sad when we know that there are but few left now that were the older ones then, and how is it now with those what were in their youth then. Many of us are now with our heads silvered over with the frosts of many winters. Our cheeks are furrowed, our bodies are bent, and time had laid his hands heavily upon most of us, and our hearts are weeping for many loved ones that have been taken from us. We are thankful that there are a goodly number yet permitted to meet on this occasion, and hope and pray that there will be many more reunions for us in the future."[1]

In 1894, Eliza was asked to speak again during the Linn County Pioneer's Reunion. This time it was held in Brownsville at what is now known as Brownsville Pioneer Park. On June 7, 1894 at 1pm, Eliza, now 56 years old, gave one more speech to the crowd of pioneers and their families. She spoke about the hardships of traveling west in the wagon

---

[1] McCormick, Linda. "1888." In *Linn County Pioneer Association, Minutes from Meetings from July 30, 1887 to June 18, 1926*, Brownsville, Oregon: Self Published, 2012. pg. 7

trains and how difficult it was to settle in a foreign place. In addition to discussing the details of the Whitman Massacre she said...

"...I see a few of my old school mates; see what changes the hand of time has done for them; years and cares have silvered their heads and furrowed their cheeks. With us yet are two of our beloved teachers, Rev. Robert Robe and Mrs. Colbert, waiting now for that summons which will say, "Good and faithful servants, their work is done," and reap the reward which await the faithful. We have mingled our joys and sorrows together and we have raised our families here. Visit the cemeteries and there you will find that most of us have loved ones who are numbered with the silent sleepers; our homes have been made vacant, our hearts are grieving for dear ones that are gone. Turn over the leaf and what meets your eye? A beautiful country wherever you go, teeming and beaming with the richest of God's blessings; a prosperous people and with all the improvements that money, art and man can make, with beautiful cities here and there, and every advantage for improving the mind and making useful men and women; church and school advantages of every description. Oh, what golden opportunities are afforded you now; our conveyances are of the best, steam boats plowing [plying] on the rivers, railroads here and there with their cars speeding and steaming through the country.*

It is no wonder that I can not find words to express my astonishment, and I can truly say,

My country 'tis of thee,
Sweet land of liberty,
Of thee I sing.

It is our duty to gather up and save all history of the settling of Oregon, for so often we see things published that are untrue, trying to put praises where they do not belong, and place blame where it should not be; and again, how frequently we see published, "another pioneer gone." There will soon be no one to answer the roll call, and then it will be some of those who came here later, on their beds of ease, rocked in the cradle of luxury after the way had been broken and the wild country civilized; they are the ones who will be trying for the praises, and telling of the many wonderful things they had done."[1]

James Warren and his family loved living near Spokane, Washington, and finally convinced his mother, Eliza, to join them. In 1896 she packed up her belongings and said goodbye to all her friends and favorite places in Brownsville. They traveled by wagon, using the old Barlow Road to cross the Cascade Mountains and crossed the Columbia River at The Dalles. They passed through the

---

[1]Spalding, Eliza. "Speech during the 1894 Linn County Pioneer's Reunion." *The Massacre* (1894). Print.

Klickitat Valley, Yakima Valley, Kititass Valley, over another mountain range and back down to the Columbia River near Wenatchee. From there they crossed the river to Waterville and the Big Bend country. Once again, they made their way to the Columbia River where Bridgeport is today. James had a ranch in the area, where they set up tents and made the best of the inconveniences in the harsh country.[1]

Eliza, along with her son, James and his family vacationed at Lake Chelan, Washington in 1908. While they were there, Eliza fell in love with the quaint and beautiful area known as Lakeside. She decided to build a home there and live out her life

Eliza's home in Chelan, Wash.
Courtesy Carol Warren Harrison

at this lovely location. She described her feelings of life at the cottage this way:

[1] Warren, Eliza Spalding. *Memoirs of the West*. Portland, Oregon: Marsh Printing Company. 1916 pg 40

"I never tire of looking at the grand and lofty mountains and the beautiful lake in all its grandeur when the white caps are being tossed up in all their fury and strength, and when it is calm and still like the soft breath of a child, and most beautiful is it when the brilliant colors of the setting sun are reflected upon the surface. It seems to me then that there is nothing more complete or grander in beauty than the scenery before my home. It is restful and it speaks in powerful language of the great work of our Creator's hand."[1]

In October of 1909, Eliza was feeling reminiscent and decided to make one more visit to her birth place. The now 71-year-old travelled by steamship and by train to Lapwai. It had to be an eye opening event for her to see all the growth of homes and cities along the way.

"And when we arrived at Lapwai there was such a feeling of sacredness entered my feelings and I looked about me. There was the cemetery and my father's grave, there was the spot where the house had stood. The bluffs, the river, the hills, where my brother and myself often played. It was no wonder that I would look, look, and look."[2]

---

[1] Warren, Eliza Spalding. *Memoirs of the West*. Portland, Oregon: Marsh Printing Company, 1916 pg 41
[2] Warren, Eliza Spalding. *Memoirs of the West*. Portland, Oregon: Marsh Printing Company, 1916 pg 42

Eliza was pleased to meet the two women who were running the mission there. They had done a wonderful job of carrying on her father's work. Miss McBeth and her niece, Miss Crawford, must have felt honored to meet Eliza in person.

After the church service that Sunday, they asked Eliza to speak to the congregation. Using an interpreter she spoke of the many changes she had seen there at the mission and how pleased she was to see that they had continued the Christian ways. She shared some stories of traveling with her father on horseback when he traveled to preach to the Nez Perce. When she had finished, the congregation sang a song to her that her father had taught them many years ago. It brought her to tears.

An old Indian told Eliza that he had taken the responsibility of caring for her father's grave. He had been friends with Rev. Spalding and told her he had felt like a brother to him. It is speculated that this is when Eliza arranged to have her mother reburied with her father where they both belonged. Consequently, Eliza Hart Spalding was buried by the Indians at Lapwai in 1913. Eliza had the opportunity to have dinner with Old Timothy's daughter-in-law while visiting in Lapwai. That visit must have been very special.[1]

Eliza reported to The Times newspaper in 1916 that she had moved from Lake Chelan to be near

[1] Warren, Eliza Spalding. *Memoirs of the West*. Portland, Oregon: Marsh Printing Company, 1916 pg 44

her son James. She said he lived near Dudley, Washington, which is now known as Tracy. A railroad hauled lumber and wheat from there. It is east of Walla Walla:

"As I have moved again, I will have to tell you my address, I am here in Walla Walla. I came here last September and should have let you know then, but my son, who lives near Dudly has been getting The Times all winter and is enjoying it.

Please send the paper to me, I want to take it as long as there are any one of the older settlers living. My, but there are few left there now to answer the last roll call.

We have had a hard winter here and more snow than any of the old settlers ever saw before. With kind regards to yourself and family and the Brownsville Times.

Mrs. Eliza Spalding Warren. 707 Lincoln Street."[1]

Eliza was listed in a telephone directory for Walla Walla, Washington, in 1916. There is a small home on the property at the time of this writing, but it is not known if that was the home she lived in or not.

It appears that Eliza must have moved again, or was with a family member during the Christmas holidays of 1916. A letter to the Editor of the

---

[1] "Eliza Spalding Writes." *The Brownsville Times*, Friday March 10, 1916.

Brownsville Times newspaper shows her in Cataldo, Idaho. In December, she wrote this letter regarding a story she saw in The Times:

"I see something in The Times Dec. 15, which I feel called upon to correct. I am not going to bring up any argument but the plain truth.

I was born in this great western country. My father and mother and Mr. and Mrs. Spalding were missionaries to the Nez Perce Indians, and crossed the plains and Rocky Mountains in company with Dr. Whitman and wife, in 1836. My father and mother settled among the Nez Perce. There is where I was born, at Lapwai, Oregon Ter. At that time, now Idaho, in the year 1837, Nov. 15, and Dr. Whitman's had a little girl baby that was a few months older than I was, but when she was two years old she was drowned, that of course left me the oldest white child living that was born in this country. I feel sorry for any one that will allow things to puff them up, but I will say this that I am glad that I am still spared to see how this great western country has developed in everything all in my lifetime. I saw Portland when there was but one log house; now see the great cities everywhere, and schools and churches. I am proud of our grand country; I am proud of the people who have made this country what it is. I can say that I am glad that I am one among a very few now that are left, who have helped to make this country what it is, and I bow my head with reverence and respect to the old Pioneer. With respect to yourself and The Times, Sincerely Yours, Mrs. Eliza Spalding Warren."[1]

"Whitman Survivor Has A Birthday" is the title of a newspaper story telling of Eliza's 80th birthday. The story says she celebrated on November 15, 1918, at her home in Kellogg, Idaho. Again, it is not known how many times Eliza moved or if this was her home, or the home of one of her children. The story went on to discuss her famous history as the daughter of an important missionary. The Brownsville Times had this news story and at the end they said:

> *"She is remarkably preserved for her 80 years, however her labors are ended and she says she is now waiting her call from on High with no dread of the future. She is the mother of 4 children, grandmother of 15 and great grandmother of 12."[2]*

Eliza passed away on June 21, 1919, in Coeur D'Alene, Idaho. The death certificate says she died from softening of the brain. In 1919 that term could have meant a number of things, such as she was

---

[1] "Oldest White Child." *The Brownsville Times*, December 29, 1916.
[2] "Eliza Spalding Warren 80 Years Oregon Resident." *The Brownsville Times*, November 23, 1918.

senile, insane, or that she had a stroke or hemorrhage.[1]

The death certificate also says the attending physician had treated her from February 1, 1919, until her death. The document was signed by her daughter, Minnie Illsley, who was living in Seattle, Washington, at the time. It is interesting to note that Minnie was not listed as one of Eliza's children in the obituary. It is possible that she personally gave the information to the newspaper and forgot to tell them her own name.[2]

PIONEER PASSES ON BEYOND
Mrs. Warren reaches the end of a long and well-spent life

The death of Mrs. Eliza Spalding Warren, which occurred at Coeur D'Alene, brings to mind the history of a very remarkable woman, with a very unusual history. She was the daughter of the Rev. Henry Harmon and Eliza Hart Spalding, and was born November 15, 1837, at Lapwai, Idaho, on the banks of the Clearwater, among the Nez Perce Indians. When nine years of age she was sent to Dr. Whitman's mission, 120 miles away, where

---

[1] Glossary of Old Medical Terms. Accessed September 9, 2014. http://www.thornber.net/medicine/html/medgloss.html.
[2] Certificate of Death for Eliza S. Warren, 21 June 1919, SL No. 26742, State of Idaho Board of Health, Vital Records Section, copy in the possession of author.

she attended school. Her only associates were Indian children, and she soon learned their ways and their language. In 1845 she made a visit on horseback with her father to the Willamette Valley, she being but eight years of age at this time. After stopping at The Dalles, they passed through Oregon City and the first settlement they saw was Portland, which consisted of one log building at that time. Her mother was the first white woman to journey to the land of the setting sun [the first to come by land]. In 1847, while the girl was attending school, and was ten years old, the Whitman Massacre took place. Mrs. Warren published a book entitled "Memoirs of the West," in which she vividly pictures her past.

In the spring of 1849 her parents moved to Linn County, near Brownsville. Her father took up a donation land claim, which included the land upon which The Times office is now located, and here they made their home and her father taught school. In January, 1851, her mother died and was the first person buried in the Brownsville cemetery. Her father died August 3, 1874, and was buried at Lapwai, Idaho where in 1913 her mother's remains also were taken and where they rest today beside her husband.

The remains arrived at Brownsville Tuesday. She leaves a great number of descendants, reaching to the fourth generation.

Mrs. Warren was an honorary member of the Rebekah Lodge at Chelan, Washington.

She leaves three children, James H. Warren, of Cataldo, Idaho, Mrs. America Crooks of Prineville, and Mrs. Lizzie Calloway, of Seattle; also thirteen grandchildren and fifteen great grandchildren. Logan Calloway, of Brownsville, is one of her grandchildren.

Funeral services were conducted at the Presbyterian Church here Wednesday afternoon by Rev. W. McLain Davis. A most eloquent and touching prayer was offered by W.P. Elmore, an old friend of Mrs. Warren. Pioneers from various parts of the country were in attendance, among them Cyrus Walker, Dr. Hill and Judge Stewart, all of Albany. The pallbearers were Henry Blakely, Amor Tussing, Lou Tycer, Bud Tycer, C.C. Cooley and James Coshow.

Mrs. Warren's life was remarkable for it's deep spiritual influence, spanning the period from the time when savage painted warriors ruled the wilderness until the

94

present, when civilization works it's wonders.[1]

Eliza Spalding Warren was buried next to her husband, Andrew Warren, on June 23, 1919, at the Brownsville Pioneer Cemetery.

Courtesy of Linda McCormick

This food pantry is located on Mountain Home Road in Brownsville. It is believed to have belonged to Andrew and Eliza Warren. The home they owned at this site burned down with some of Eliza's possessions in 1973.

[1] "Pioneer Passes on Beyond." *The Brownsville Times.* June 27, 1919.

Henry Hart Spalding
An Illustrated History of the State of Washington
Lewis Publishing Co.

Henry Hart Spalding
1839 – 1898

Henry Hart Spalding was born at the Spalding Mission at Lapwai in the Oregon Country on November 24, 1839. Henry was the second child of Henry and Eliza. His middle name comes from his mother's maiden name.

Henry was about nine years old when the family traveled to their new home in Brownsville, Oregon. A young schoolmate of Henry's, Margaret Blakely [Smith], reported how strict his father was as a school teacher regardless of whether he was dealing with his own child or not.

"I saw Spalding punish his own son one day at school. We were playing outside and Henry Spalding made one of the girls cry. His father called him in and cut a heavy hazel stick. He split it about half way up and put it on Henry's nose like a pair of pincers. It pinched so tight that it made the boys nose bleed, and in that state his father sent him off home, crying as he went". [1]

When Henry was older, he was sent to Tualatin Academy in Forest Grove for his high school education. A historian at Pacific University, formerly Tualatin Academy, found some records at the school showing that Henry was a student there in 1853, 1855, and 1856. The records are not complete so it is assumed that it is possible he was also there in 1854.

Soon after finishing school, Henry moved to Mount Idaho, Idaho, where he devoted his energies to the business of packing and hauling freight. Henry married Lucy A. Knifong in 1868. Sadly, she died only two years later in 1870. There is little written about this marriage. [2] At some point, he moved to Grangeville, Idaho, where he helped start the Charity Grange #15 in 1874. The grange is still a prosperous organization today. [3]

[1] Mrs. Margaret Blakley Smith. Interview by Leslie Haskins. *W.P.A. Works Project* 1937. Print.
[2] "Henry Hart Spalding." Find A Grave. Accessed September 16, 2014.
[3] "Mary Warren Spalding Lives Happily in Sunset Years at Old Almota Home." *Unknown.* 1936

Henry married Mary (Muddy) Catherine Warren (no known relation to Henry's brother-in-law Andrew) on March 31, 1875, in her parent's home in Touchet, Washington. It is very possible that Henry met his bride through the bride's brother, Felix Warren. Warren was one of the most well known stage drivers west of the Rockies and hauled freight in the same area Henry did. It is possible that Henry may have worked for Felix.[1]

There is evidence that indicates Henry owned 155 acres in Prescott, Washington, which ended up becoming the hub of the Oregon Railway and Navigation Company.[2] Since that railroad traveled through Almota, Washington, and picked up freight there, Henry could have been enticed to relocate to Almota by the people at Prescott and to settle down with his new wife.

Henry's sister, Eliza, told a story about when he first arrived at Almota. Before he brought his bride to live there, he had encountered some trouble with the Indians. They stole his horses and disrupted their camp site. A few days later, Henry's brother-in-law, Andrew Warren, pulled a gun on an Indian. Henry jumped in and convinced the Indian to leave. Before he left, the Indian asked him his name. Henry's answer completely changed the Indian's

[1] "Felix Warren." Idaho Genealogy. Accessed September 24, 2014. http://www.idahogenealogy.com/nezperce/felix_warren.htm.
[2] "Land Patent." *Bureau of Land Management / General Land Office*. U.S. Dept of the Interior. Web. 25 Sep 2014. <http://www.glorecords.blm.gov/results/default.aspx?searchCriteria=type=patent|st=WA|cty=|ln=spaulding|fn=henry|mn=h|dn=228|sp=true|sw=true|sadv=false>.

attitude. He asked if Henry was related to Reverend Henry Spalding. When Henry told him he was his son, the Indian brought back the stolen horses and the Indians never bothered them again.[1]

The new couple settled on some fertile land that Henry had bought from the only two men who lived there at the time, L. M. Ringer and Jack Turner. The property was along the Snake River and the two men supplied driftwood to the passing steamboats that went up and down the river. The land was at a bend in the river, and the floating wood got caught there. It was a perfect business. The riverbank at that location was flat and close to the river. The Oregon Railway and Navigation Company also established a landing and discharging place there, which made it an important shipping point for the country north of the Snake River.[2]

Mr. Ringer and Mr. Turner stayed at Almota and helped Henry build it into a thriving community. In 1876, the first shipment of Whitman County wheat was shipped by steamer on the Snake River from Almota to Portland. Henry opened a warehouse in 1876, and Mr. Ringer opened a store when the town was laid out in 1877. Eventually, liberal inducements were offered to businessmen and a couple hotels, two more warehouses, a grist mill, several shops, a school house and many homes

[1]Warren, Eliza Spalding. *Memoirs of the West*. Portland, Oregon: Marsh Printing Company, 1916 pg 37

[2] Gilbert, Frank T. Historic Sketches of Walla Walla, Whitman, Columbia and Garfield Counties - Washington & Umatilla County, Oregon. Portland, Oregon: 1882. 445. Print.

were built. Henry became the postmaster, which he probably learned from his father back in Brownsville, Oregon. In a few short months the area grew to become the thriving town of Almota.[1]

Henry helped build one of the first hotels in Almota, and lived in it with his wife early on. Mary reported later that Rev. Eells, who worked as a missionary along with the Rev. Spalding, traveled through Almota once and stopped to hold a church service at the hotel. They were also known to hold parties and dances at the hotel. Henry made his blacksmith shop into a small school room and, by 1884, they built a new school for 42 students.[2]

The hotel owned by the Spaldings
Courtesy of the Dave Peterson Collection

Henry and Mary had nine children with only three living to adulthood. Henry Dolph (Dolph) died at

[1] Gilbert, Frank T. Historic Sketches of Walla Walla, Whitman, Columbia and Garfield Counties - Washington & Umatilla County, Oregon. Portland, Oregon: 1882. 445. Print.
[2] *Told by the Pioneers*. Mrs. Mary C. Spalding. 3. A Washington Pioneer Project. 1938. Web. http://www.sos.wa.gov/legacy/images/publications/.

age 16 from spinal meningitis, Ralph died around 18-years-old and Mary C. died in her 20s. Their oldest son, Horace Hart Spalding, married Belle Russell and had two children. Frederick Eugene (Eugene) Spalding married Katherine Bean and had two children. Marcus Whitman Spalding married Eileen Wade and had one daughter.

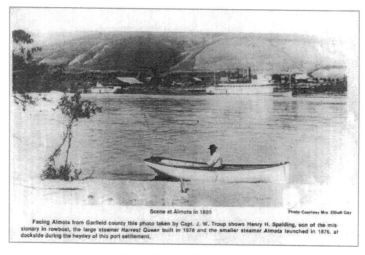

Scene at Almota in 1880   Photo Courtesy Mrs. Elliott Gay

Facing Almota from Garfield county this photo taken by Capt. J. W. Troup shows Henry H. Spalding, son of the missionary in rowboat, the large steamer *Harvest Queen* built in 1878 and the smaller steamer *Almota* launched in 1876, at dockside during the heyday of this port settlement.

Henry Hart Spalding in a boat
Courtesy of the Dave Peterson Collection

Henry's farm was known as one of the most flourishing stock, wheat, and fruit farms for miles around. He owned 1,200 acres of land including an excellent prune orchard, a general orchard with a variety of trees, the Almota flouring mill, and a warehouse. His home was known as one of the finest in the area. For 20 years he was postmaster at Almota, was involved with the local school and, for many years, was president of the school board. He was a well respected and involved citizen of Almota.

The account books for Henry's businesses are located today at Washington State University in Pullman. The books show transactions in products and services, including grain, produce, wood, general merchandise, blacksmithing, and shipping. The business account books in the archives date from 1877 to 1892. The name in the check register was then Marcus Spalding (his son), which includes a bill of sale for the Almota store in 1922.

Henry died from injuries during a fire in his home on March 22, 1898, at the age of 58. Apparently, Henry was carrying a mattress out of his burning house and jumped off a back porch and suffered internal injuries. He died two days later. One of the great losses in the fire was a Bible his mother gave him before she died that had personal messages written to him from her.[1]

Eliza Spalding Warren wrote in her book *"Memoirs of the West"* about Henry's death and shared this text from a newspaper:

> *Buried in flowers. Impressive ceremonies at funeral of the late Henry Spalding. The gathering of the late Henry Spalding at Almota, Thursday afternoon of last week, was a splendid tribute to the worth of the dead pioneer. Six hundred friends followed all that was mortal of a brave and honorable man to the last resting place. The floral offerings were profuse and elaborate.*

---

[1] "Mary Warren Spalding Lives Happily in Sunset Years at Old Almota Home." *Unknown.*1936

Among wreaths and flowers were those from his various lodges, the Knights of the Pythias, A.O.U.W., the Red Men, the Rathbones and others. [1]

A newspaper journalist, Dan W. Greenburg, shared about his friend, Henry Hart Spalding, in an editorial he wrote for the Spalding Centennial in 1936. He wrote:

...That he inherited the pioneering spirit of his parents and was agriculturally and horticulturally inclined is known to all who ever visited the beautiful Spalding estate at Almota...His passing was a tragedy throughout Whitman County and the Lewiston country...He was a capable and energetic business man and in addition to marketing fruit from his famous orchard, maintained a large grain warehouse and bought and shipped grain. It was then one of the important landing places of the steamboats operating on the river between Riparia and Lewiston... [2]

During the Lewiston, Idaho, Spalding Centennial in 1936, the newspapers were filled with stories about the Spalding and Whitman missions and Rev. Spalding and his accomplishments. Unfortunately, clippings collected by Margaret Carey were cut out

---

[1] Warren, Eliza Spalding. *Memoirs of the West.* Portland, Oregon: Marsh Printing Company, 1916 pg 38

[2] Greenburg, Dan W. "Spalding Centennial." *Lewiston Morning Tribune?* [Lewiston, Idaho] May 1936, Print.

of the newspapers without revealing what paper
and what the date was. It is assumed it was in the
Lewiston Tribune where the other stories were
found.

In one of the news clippings dated March 21, 1936,
there is a story about Henry's 17-year-old
granddaughter, Joanne Spalding, who was involved
with the centennial event. It was reported that she
was the first person in years to use the printing
press Rev. Henry Spalding had shipped to the
Spalding Mission in 1839. This was the first
printing press in the Northwest and was used by
Rev. Spalding to print Indian translations of the
Bible and hymn books for use of the missionaries.
Joanne used the printing press to print out an
invitation to President Franklin Roosevelt inviting
him to be present at the Centennial celebration. The
invitation read:

Idaho Spalding Centennial Association
Lewiston, Idaho
March 21, 1936

My dear Mr. President,
In recognition of the honor due the pioneers who 100 years ago made the arduous trip across the continent over the Rocky Mountains into the Pacific Northwest carrying the torch of civilization which eventually resulted in the acquisition of the vast Oregon country by the United States, the people of Idaho cordially invite you to open the Idaho Spalding Centennial celebration to be held in Lewiston, first capital of Idaho, on May 7, 8, 9, and 10.

You will be interested to know that this invitation was printed by Miss Joan Spalding, great grand-daughter of Rev. Henry and Eliza Spalding, who established the first home in Idaho and in whose honor the celebration is held, on the first printing press ever brought into the west. This press in use in the Sandwich Islands was brought to the Lapwai Mission, founded by the Spaldings in Idaho, in 1836 and was used to print tracts from the Bible in the Nez Perce Indian language so that the message of God could be given to the tribe.
Expressing our appreciation for your interest in this historic observance, we have the honor to remain
Faithfully yours,

The President declined the offer.

In another clipping, likely dated in May of 1936, there is a photo of Miss Joanne Spalding (great granddaughter of Rev. Henry Harmon Spalding) and her sister-in-law, Mrs. Dolph Spalding, and an explanation that they were invited to a Spokane Chamber of Commerce noon luncheon. It was announced at the luncheon that Miss Spalding, a senior at Lewis & Clark High School, would be the Princess Spokane at the Idaho Spalding Centennial at Lewiston May 7 to 10.

Henry Hart Spalding is buried in the Spalding Cemetery near Almota in Whitman County. Buried with him in the small cemetery are his wife, Mary Catherine, and children Glen, Ralph, Harry, Effie and Henry (Dolph).

Spalding Cemetery in Almota, Washington
Courtesy of Arthur Allen Moore III

Mrs. Martha J. Spalding Wigle

Courtesy of the Bowman Museum

Martha Jane Spalding Wigle
1845 – 1924

Martha Jane Spalding was born at the Spalding Mission at Lapwai, in the Oregon Country, on March 20, 1845. She was the third child of Henry and Eliza Spalding.

After she attended school at her father's Spalding School in Brownsville, she traveled to Forest Grove for her high school education at the Tualatin Academy. Records found her listed there in 1856 and 1857. A number of other local young people from the Brownsville area went to the Tualatin Academy as well.

Martha's Brownsville friend, Luella Colbert Robnett, reported in an interview that Martha was quite the horse woman and even competed in horse exhibitions at the fairs.[1]

There seems to be a mystery about the marriage of Martha and William (Bill) Wigle. People who were interviewed many years ago claim her father did not approve of the relationship, so she eloped with Bill. The story told is they rode by horseback and "eloped up The Gap". The Gap was also known as the Territorial Road and ran south between chasms in the foothills all the way to Eugene. They say her father gave chase on horseback. Bill had family who lived on Belts Road, also up The Gap, and they could have been heading there.

The reason for the mystery is because evidence shows that Martha moved with her family in 1859 to Touchet, Washington. She would have been about 13 or 14 years old and her father would have deemed her too young to be married. It is also known that Martha and Bill were married on April 15, 1860 in The Dalles, Oregon by Justice of the Peace, John E. Broughton. So, it makes sense that before the family moved to Washington, Martha and Bill may have attempted to run away, but were stopped by her father or someone else. Considering

---

[1] Mrs.Luella Colbert, Robnett. Interview by Leslie Haskins. *W.P.A. Works Project*. Approx 1936. Page 117

Henry and his entire family were not in Brownsville in 1860, this makes for a reasonable account of what probably happened.

Another detail that adds credence to the synopsis is that the 1860 Agriculture Census shows that Bill had 60 improved acres and 100 unimproved acres in Touchet, Washington. The document showed that he had three horses and 10 milk cows. He also had wheat and oats. Nearby were the Spaldings and the Warrens.[1]

It is said they lived in Brownsville for a time before moving away, but it is not known as a fact. There is evidence that Bill owned some land near his family down The Gap, and he was assessed a tax from the I.R.S. in 1869 for cattle.[2] He also was listed as owning this land in 1878.[3]

Documentation was found that shows they later had property on Willow Creek near the town of Ione, Oregon (not far from Heppner).[4] In a relative's interview, it was said the Wigles sold that property and moved to The Dalles.[5] It is not known when they made that move or how long they lived in The Dalles, but it was long enough to make lifelong friends. After they moved away, a number of

[1] "1860 Agriculture Census - search for William Wiggle." *Ancestry.com.* Ancestry.com, Web. 14 Dec 2014.
[2] "U.S IRS Tax Assessment ." *Ancestry.com.* N.p., Web. 13 Dec 2014.
[3] "All U.S., Indexed County Land Ownership Maps, 1860-1918." *Ancestry.com.* Ancestry.com, Web. 14 Dec 2014.
[4] "Patent Details." U.S. Bureau of Land Management. U.S. Department of Interior. Web. 24 Oct 2014. <www.glorecords.blm.gov>.
[5] Wigle, Mr. Ed. Interview by Leslie L. Haskin. "Mr. Ed Wigle." *W.P.A. Interviews.* Approx 1936. Vol. 8 page 7

newspaper stories in The Dalles Daily Chronicle mentioned that they came back to visit friends.

The Wigles had five children. They were John Henry, Ida Ellen (died at 9 months old), Minnie Laura Wigle Larwood, Albert Lee (Lee), and Eliza Lorena Wigle Milliorn.

William Wigle
Courtesy of the Bowman Museum

The 1880 census showed that Martha was living with her sister, Eliza Warren, in Brownsville, along with her children Minnie (14 years old), Lee (11 years old), and Eliza (five years old), but there is no mention of Bill. It is possible he was helping his brother-in-law, Andrew Warren, on a cattle drive along with other cattlemen from the Prineville area.

Bill was in the stock business so he could have taken his own cattle on the drive. Also in 1880, there was some kind of legal action held in Walla Walla, Washington, between Bill and a Chinese man named Lai Poy. It was documented as a civil case with collection/account as the cause. It isn't known if he was present at the hearing.[1]

In approximately 1886, the Wigle family moved to Camp Creek near Prineville, Oregon.[2] There is evidence that shows that Bill operated The Dalles & Prineville Stage Company at least until 1892.

The Dalles to Prineville Stage Co.
Courtesy of the Bowman Museum

[1] "Walla Walla Frontier Justice-Digital Archives." *Washington State Archives*. Washington State Archives, n.d. Web. 14 Dec 2014. <http://www.digitalarchives.wa.gov/Record/View/AB12FB42B2C964852 3538C26AA7236AD>.
[2] "Patent Details." U.S. Bureau of Land Management. U.S. Department of Interior. Web. 24 Oct 2014. <www.glorecords.blm.gov>.

The Prineville area had serious problems with vigilantes during this time so the mail and freight business was a risky job.[1]

Bill died in Prineville, Oregon on August 2, 1913. It is assumed that Martha moved into town after Bill's death. The ranch land the Wigles owned was flooded long after they were gone when the Bureau of Land Reclamation installed a dam on the Crooked River and created the popular Prineville Reservoir in 1961.[2]

The local Prineville newspaper printed Bill's obituary:

Obituary of William Wigle

William Wigle died at his home in Prineville, Saturday, August 2, at the age of 77 years, 9 months and 22 days.

Mr. Wigle was born in Illinois, October 10, 1835. He crossed the plains in 1852 and settled in Linn County. In 1860 he married Martha Spalding. In 1887 Mr. and Mrs. Wigle moved to Crook County where they have since resided. Mr. Wigle had been a sufferer from a complication of diseases for several years but insisted on moving about until the very last. His familiar figure and

[1]"When the Vigilantes Ruled Prineville." *Offbeat Oregon*. 1 Jan. 2012. Web. 14 Jan. 2015. <http://offbeatoregon.com/1211d-lynching-kicked-off-vigilante-rule-in-prineville.html>.
[2]"Prineville Reservoir." *Wikipedia*. N.p.. Web. 24 Oct 2014. <http://en.wikipedia.org/wiki/Prineville_Reservoir>.

kind greeting will be missed by his many friends who met him each day. He was a good husband, kind father and loyal friend, and was always ready to help those in need.

He leaves a wife and four children, all of whom were present at the funeral. The children are – John Wigle of Prineville, Mrs. Larwood of Eugene, Lee Wigle of Portland, Mrs. Milliorn of Eugene.

Mr. Wigle was buried from his family residence in Prineville, Sunday, August 3.

Almost exactly a year after his father's death, their son Lee was met with an untimely death that must have devastated his newly widowed mother. Lee and his wife took 40 head of cattle to sell in the far reaches of the Yukon in Alaska. He had been having some health issues and they thought the cold air might be good for him. While they were the farthest away, he fell ill and his wife hurried to get him home. When they docked at the town of Tanana on the Yukon River, a doctor was called. Lee died on the bow of the boat. His wife had to wait a number of weeks for a coffin to be delivered so his body could be transported the rest of the way home. It took over a month to bring Lee back home to Oregon. He was buried at Juniper Haven Cemetery in Prineville, Oregon.[1]

---

[1] "Brings Body of Husband Through Desolate Alaska." *East Oregonian* 7 Sept. 1914, Daily Evening Edition ed.: 5. Print.

Martha Jane Spalding Wigle
Courtesy of the Bowman Museum

The 1920 census showed that Martha was living with her daughter Eliza in the town of Goshen in Lane County. Martha died on December 2, 1924 at 79-years-old and was buried alongside her husband at the Juniper Haven Cemetery in Prineville, Oregon.

Martha's daughter Eliza Wigle Milliorn
Courtesy of the Bowman Museum

Amelia Lorene Spalding Brown
Courtesy Linn County Historical Museum

Amelia Lorene Spalding Brown (Millie)
1846 – 1889

Amelia was the fourth child of Henry and Eliza Spalding and was only one year old when the family fled from the Indian country. She was born on December 12, 1846, and was known as Millie to the people around her.

Once the family was settled, her father would be called to preach in faraway places, and he would let Millie ride in front of him on his horse until she got too big, and then he had her ride behind him. Millie fast became famous for her singing abilities, and people loved it when Henry brought her along.[1]

Little Millie was only five years old when her mother passed away. When she was seven, her father remarried, which must have been a big change for such a little girl. Rachel, her new mother figure, apparently was not very good at domestic housekeeping, as described in previous chapters, but she was a well meaning and caring person.

As with the other Spalding children, Millie went to her father's school along with the Courtney's, Blakely's, Brown's and other pioneer families.

Millie's older sister, Eliza, married Andrew Warren at 16 years old in 1854 and brought young Millie to the Warren farm to help do household chores. There is speculation that here is when Millie first hurt her back, as she and Eliza were left to carry heavy buckets of water from the well or Warren Creek and to find and haul firewood.[2]

In 1859, the entire Spalding family followed Eliza and her husband, and moved to Touchet, Washington. Eliza and Andrew did not stay long, as they moved back to the Warren Ranch on Mountain Home Road in 1861. It is unknown if Millie came back with the Warrens at that time.

---

[1] Carey, Margaret. "The Forgotten Daughter." *The Times* 2 Feb. 1978, Past Times sec. Print.
[2] Mrs. Lizzie Reinhart, Weber. Interview by Leslie L. Haskin. "Mrs. Lizzie Reinhart Webber." *W.P.A.Project*. 1936? Print.

It makes sense that because of the relationship Rev. Spalding had with Hugh Leeper Brown (the Spalding property was part of a land split with Mr. Brown), and the fact that the children of the area were taught at Rev. Spalding's schoolhouse, John Brown and Millie were probably friends, even though he was 15 years older. In any case, they were married on November 12, 1863, when she was only 16 years old.

The 1870 census shows John Brown with his wife Amelia, and their two daughters, five-year-old Florence and three-year-old Loretta, living in the Sand Ridge Precinct. In researching where exactly the Sand Ridge Precinct was it was learned that:

> *Sand Ridge - This was never a town, but was of historical mention because of the 1855 attempt to change the county seat from Albany to Sand Ridge. A committee composed of William Cyrus, H. J. C. Averill and Luther White were appointed to make a survey and select a site as near to the center of the county as possible. The vote, taken in June of 1855, had Sand Ridge a clear winner, but in 1856 another vote was taken and Albany won. Sand Ridge is located west of Peterson's Butte, in the Lebanon area.*[1]

It is assumed that the name below the Browns in the census was a neighbor. In this case the neighbor was William Templeton and his family, that

---

[1]"Old Towns." *Linn County, Oregon Genealogy & History*. Web. 16 Oct. 2014. <http://www.genealogytrails.com/ore/linn/towns/oldtowns.html>.

included his widowed daughter Matilda Foster, and her 3-year-old son, Alexander (Clyde) Foster. Matilda's husband had been killed when he fell into a tank of hot dye at the Brownsville Woolen Mill. Years later, in 1890, Clyde married Loretta Brown.

After Millie's mother passed away, Rev. Spalding divided his land so all four children could have an equal number of acres. Millie's share was on the west of the long part of the property. In 1865, three years after they married, her husband John purchased 246 more acres from Rev. Spalding and Rachel. By this time Rev. Spalding had moved back to the Indian country. In the description of the deed, dated August 21, 1865, it says this land included the three acres or more of the orchard, the house and well. It also included one and a half acres that included the barn and free use of the pasture for two cows and one horse.

They engaged in farming and raising livestock. John was also financially involved with the local woolen and flour mills.

It is recorded that John built the beautiful home in Brownsville, we know today as Atavista House, in 1876, but there seems to be some question if that is the correct year.

The 1880 census had a note to the side of Amelia's name that she had "disease of the spine". Because of her health problems Millie was only able to enjoy the house in full for a very short time.

Millie's home known today as Atavista Farm.
Courtesy of Atavista Farm

John and Millie had five children, two of which died after childbirth. Their children were Florence Lillian Brown Waters (died at age 23), Loretta (Retta) Adelma Brown Foster West, and Malcom Earl (Earl) Brown.

While Rev. Spalding was on his famous trip back east in 1871, he was sent word that Millie was very ill. He left Chicago on July 3 by train and then took a stage from Sacramento arriving home on August 14. He was so concerned about his youngest daughter that he stayed at her bedside until she gave birth to baby girl on September 21. The baby died the next day.[1] The year before, she lost a son at birth. Millie mourned those two babies for the rest of her life, and she wrote about them in her diary. Despite her intense pain and confinement to bed, Millie Brown gave birth to her youngest son, Earl, while she was bedbound. He was the only child born in the house we call Atavista.

Earl and Tessie Brown
Courtesy Linn County Historical Museum

Millie was an invalid for over 20 years with a badly overlapped spine that eventually confined her to

[1] Clifford Merrill Drury, *Henry Harmon Spalding* (Idaho. The Caxton Printers Ltd. 1936) pg 397

her bed. In an interview with Millie's caregiver, Lizzie Reinhart Webber, she reported that Millie could not even turn herself over in bed or raise up one of her knees to change position. Some people have speculated that Millie hurt her back by hard work when she helped Eliza on the ranch years before, in a horse riding accident, or in childbirth. It would make sense that all of these could have played a role in her physical disability.[1]

Lizzie worked for Millie for approximately two years and was sometimes the only person she had to talk to. There are sad stories told about Millie in Lizzie's interview. Assuming the stories are true, the Brown family and Millie's own sister, Eliza, treated her poorly and refused to visit with her when she was laid up in bed. It was said that John Brown's sister, Missouri, would not let her husband, John Tycer, stop and visit Millie when he rode past the house. So, he would whistle gospel songs that he knew Millie enjoyed hoping she would hear him. When John Tycer died, Millie sent Missouri a letter and soon she came to visit Millie and apologized.[2]

John and Millie had an interesting financial arrangement according to Lizzie and others. Millie inherited her father's farm. John purchased more of Rev. Spalding's land, yet John would only allow Millie to spend money that was earned on her

[1]Mrs. Lizzie Reinhart, Weber. Interview by Leslie L. Haskin. "Mrs. Lizzie Reinhart Webber." *W.P.A.Project*. 1936? Print.
[2] Mrs. Lizzie Reinhart, Weber. Interview by Leslie L. Haskin. "Mrs. Lizzie Reinhart Webber." *W.P.A.Project*. 1936? Print.

inherited land (the farm). Because the farm property did not make much profit she ended up sewing clothing for her children, and even took orders from others. She had a mare and would sell the colts for spending money.

One of the saddest stories told by Lizzie was that John would not allow Millie to spend money on underwear. Millie would end up with the worn out, dirty, and shrunken underwear that John himself wore:

> *"Millie told me to bring her John's old underwear and she cut it down and worked it over and made some for herself. It kept on shrinking until she could scarcely get it on, and then there was seams around the waist where she had cut it down which hurt her back. I said to her, "It's a shame for you to wear these things that hurt you when Brown has plenty of money laid away". John Brown heard me. He said "What's that? What are you storming around for? Spit out what's eating you." I told him just exactly what I said. I told him, "It's a shame for that poor thing to lie there suffering for want of decent clothes when you have more money than you can use." The next time that he went to town he came home and threw a big box on her bed. She said, "Why John, I didn't send for anything." He said, "Open it and see." I handed it to her. She couldn't reach it. He knew she couldn't. The box was full of the very nicest underwear.*

Millie asked me for her account book. She looked in it and said, "I haven't any money now to pay for them." Do you know what that man did? He took them back to the store and told the storekeeper that Millie said they weren't good enough.

Millie said to me, "Don't tell anyone about this." I went to the store after that to buy some things and the storekeeper said to me, "What kind of woman is that Mrs. Brown? She must be a queer one. Her husband got the very best underwear and she said it wasn't good enough." I just stood and looked at him. I had promised Millie not to tell, and I didn't."[1]

Apparently, Eliza had always assumed she would own her father's farm property, but Henry wanted Millie to have it. Again, in the Lizzie Weber interview, she shares an incident about this subject. Eliza had finally come for a visit after a long absence, but really didn't have much to say to Millie. She came for a cutting of a grape plant (which may be the grapes still growing on the property today). When Eliza left, Millie shared some information with Lizzie. Years before, Rev. Spalding had a talk with Millie:

"Millie, I have made my will, and you are to have the home place." I said, "Oh no Father, Eliza has always wanted that place.

---

[1] Mrs. Lizzie Reinhart, Weber. Interview by Leslie L. Haskin. "Mrs. Lizzie Reinhart Webber." *W.P.A.Project.* 1936? Print.

Give me the hill farm and it will be alright with me. I love that hill place. I always liked the woods and the running brooks and I would be so happy there." He said, "No, Eliza gets that. When Eliza began going with Warren I begged her not to marry him. I told her that he drank and didn't care for anything but drinking and begged her not to do it, but she would have her own way. Now, you can have the home place and she can take her man and live back in the woods. That is the only place for her and her drunken sot." I never asked my father for anything about the place. I never thought of it. I said to my father, "But Eliza wants this place, she always has." Father said, "What I have done I have done. Eliza had her way in things that I asked her not to do. Now she cannot have the home farm. I will tell her myself."[1]

The hill place that Millie refers to is an area known to old-timers as Amelia. Today it is north of Kirk Avenue near the end of Spaulding Way.

Amelia - H. H. Spaulding laid out this town in 1858, near the present site of Brownsville. In 1876 the Oregon Legislative Assembly named this site North Brownsville.[2]

---

[1] Mrs. Lizzie Reinhart, Weber. Interview by Leslie L. Haskin. "Mrs. Lizzie Reinhart Webber." *W.P.A.Project*. 1936? Print.
[2] "Old Towns." *Linn County, Oregon Genealogy & History*. Web. 16 Oct. 2014. <http://www.genealogytrails.com/ore/linn/towns/oldtowns.html>.

Four months before Millie died on November 25, 1889, her oldest daughter, Florence Waters, died at almost 24-years-old. Millie's young son, Earl, was almost three when his mother passed away. Amelia's daughter, Retta, inherited the farm, but after divorcing her husband, Clyde Foster, she sold it.

Millie kept a diary and filled it with poetry from famous poets and some of her own work. A few of her musings were very sad, as she shared her feelings of being an invalid and the loss of her two babies. The diary is now in the possession of Terry and Sharon McCoy, current owners of the Atavista House.

If you do not lighten your own home, your light is gone out. [This was found in Millie's diary]

A quilt made by Millie while bedridden
Courtesy of the Oregon Historical Society

Afterword

The process of writing this book was very similar to researching one's own genealogy. The difference was I had no family stories passed down through time like you might in your own family. I had to depend on clues and bits of information found near and far that helped put the information into one complete story. There are gaps in time and questions in fact that make this an incomplete work. I did my best to confirm and prove the information I have shared here. If a reader finds an error in fact, or would like to add information to the story, I would welcome that. My gift to you is one book with information you will not find gathered together anywhere else. I hope you are inspired to research for yourself who some of our early pioneers were and the legacy they left for us.

Spalding Family Tree

Henry Harmon Spalding 1803 – 1874
Eliza Hart Spalding 1807 – 1851
Rachel Jahonet (Jane) Smith 1808 – 1880

Eliza Spalding Warren 1837 – 1919
Andrew Jackson Warren 1832 – 1886
1. America Jane Warren Crooks 1856 – 1954
   Joseph Henry Crooks 1843 – 1918

2. Martha Elizabeth Warren Calloway 1859 – 1882
   James Granville Calloway 1848 – 1913

3. Amelia (Minnie) Warren Illsley 1862 –1942
   Fred Forrest Illsley 1859 – 1924

4. James (Jimmy) Henry Warren 1866 –1935
   Nancy Jane Wiseman 1868 – 1948

Henry Hart Spalding 1839 – 1898
Lucy Knifong 1848 – 1870
Mary Catherine Warren 1854 – 1941

1. Glen Spalding

2. Ralph Spalding died at 18

3. Mary C Spalding d – 1901

4. Harry Spalding 1877 – 1878

5. Effie Edith Spalding 1879 – 1880

6. Horace Hart Spalding 1881 –
   Belle Russell

7. Henry Dolph (Dolph) Spalding 1889 – 1905

8. Frederick Eugene (Eugene) Spalding 1885? – 1928
   Katherine Bean

9. Marcus Whitman Spalding 1897 – 1975
   Eileen Wade 1899 – 1970

Martha Jane Spalding Wigle 1845 – 1924
William (Bill) Wigle 1835 – 1913

1. John Henry Wigle 1862 – 1949
   May J. 1869 – 1929

2. Ida Ellen Wigle 1863 – 1864

3. Minnie Laura Wigle Larwood 1865 – 1931
   Thomas H. Larwood 1893 – 1967

4. Albert Lee (Lee) Wigle 1868 – 1914
   Lola M. Wilkins
   Agnes M. Boyd

5. Eliza Lorena Wigle Milliorn 1875 – 1944
   Frank Byron (Barney) Milliorn

Amelia (Millie) Lorene Spalding Wigle 1846 – 1889
John Brown 1831 – 1894

1. Florence Lillian Brown Waters 1865 – 1889
   John Waters

2. Loretta (Retta) Adelma Brown Foster West 1867
   Alexander (Clyde) Foster 1866 – 1942
   Ossian J. West

3. Infant son Brown d –April 1870

4. Infant daughter Brown d –September 1871

5. Malcom Earl (Earl) Brown 1887 – 1960
   Tessie Carla Johnson

Bibliography

Books:

Clifford Merrill Drury, *Henry Harmon Spalding* (Idaho, The Caxton Printers Ltd. 1936)

Warren, Eliza Spalding. *Memoirs of the West*. Portland, Oregon: Marsh Printing Company, 1916

Erwin N. Thompson, *Shallow Grave at Waiilatpu: The Sagers' West*, (Portland, Oregon: Glass-Dahlstrom Printers, 1969)

Lansing, Ronald B. *Juggernaut, the Whitman Massacre Trial.* : Oregon Historical Society, 1993.

Websites:

"Spalding Memorial." *Internet Archive*. N.p.. Web. 12 Jan 2015. <http://archive.org/stream/spaldingmemorialcad00spal/spaldingme morialcad00spal_djvu.txt>.

Miranda, G., & Read, R. (2000). *Splendid Audacity: The story of Pacific University*. Forest Grove, OR: Pacific University. Sept. 22, 2013 < http://commons.pacificu.edu/mono/3/#>

Tate, Cassandra, *"Whitman-Spalding missionary party arrives at Fort Vancouver on September 12, 1836".* "Westward Ho" Feb. 2011, Historylink.org. Sept. 22, 2013 <http://www.historylink.org/index.cfm?DisplayPage=output.cfm& file_id=9700>

Whitman Mission National Historic Site, *"The Spalding & Whitman Missions*
A brief chronology of the Spalding's & Whitman's in the Northwest." Sept. 22, 2013 <http://www.3rd1000.com/history3/fur/furposts/ww_whitman.htm >

"Founding Mother: Eliza Hart Spalding and the
Spalding Mission.", *Women in Idaho History,* May 2011, Sept. 22,
2013
<http://womeninidahohistory.wordpress.com/2011/05/02/eliza-
hart-spalding/>

Filer, Charlotte C., *"Pacific Profiles: 1849 – 1885",* 1981, Pacific
University, Sept. 22,2013
<http://www.pacificu.edu/library/documents/pacificprofiles.pdf>

Glossary of Old Medical Terms. Accessed September 9, 2014.
<http://www.thornber.net/medicine/html/medgloss.html.

"Henry Hart Spalding." Find A Grave. Accessed September 16,
2014. http://www.findagrave.com/cgi-
bin/fg.cgi?page=gr&GSln=spalding&GSfn=Henry&GSmn=hart&
GSbyrel=all&GSdyrel=in&GScntry=4&GSob=n&GRid=5299895
2&df=all&.

Told by the Pioneers. Mrs. Mary C. Spalding. 3. A Washington
Pioneer Project, 1938. 21. Web.
<http://www.sos.wa.gov/legacy/images/publications/SL_unitedpio
neersv3/SL_unitedpioneersv3.pdf>.

"Land Patent." *Bureau of Land Management / General Land
Office.* U.S. Dept of the Interior. Web.
<http://www.glorecords.blm.gov/results/default.aspx?searchCriteri
a=type=patent|st=WA|cty=|ln=spaulding|fn=henry|mn=h|dn=228|s
p=true|sw=true|sadv=false>.

"1860 Agriculture Census - search for William Wiggle."
Ancestry.com. Ancestry.com, Web.

"Old Towns"
http://www.genealogytrails.com/ore/linn/towns/oldtowns.html

"U.S IRS Tax Assessment ." *Ancestry.com.* N.p., Web.

"All U.S., Indexed County Land Ownership Maps, 1860-1918."
Ancestry.com. Ancestry.com, Web.

"Walla Walla Frontier Justice-Digital Archives." *Washington State
Archives.* Washington State Archives, n.d. Web. 14 Dec 2014.
<http://www.digitalarchives.wa.gov/Record/View/AB12FB42B2C
9648523538C26AA7236AD>.

"Prineville Reservoir." *Wikipedia.* N.p.. Web. 24 Oct 2014.
<http://en.wikipedia.org/wiki/Prineville_Reservoir>.

"When the Vigilantes Ruled Prineville." *Offbeat Oregon.* 1 Jan.
2012. Web. 14 Jan. 2015. <http://offbeatoregon.com/1211d-
lynching-kicked-off-vigilante-rule-in-prineville.html>.

Newspaper:

"Eliza Spalding Writes." *The Brownsville Times*, Friday March 10,
1916.

"Oldest White Child." *The Brownsville Times*, December 29, 1916.

"Eliza Spalding Warren 80 Years Oregon Resident." *The
Brownsville Times*, November 23, 1918.

"Pioneer Passes on Beyond." *The Brownsville Times*, June 27,
1919.

"Brings Body of Husband Through Desolate Alaska." *East
Oregonian* 7 Sept. 1914, Daily Evening Edition ed.: 5. Print.

Private Document:

Mrs. Elias, Marsters. Interview by Leslie Haskins. *W.P.A. Works
Project* 08 Nov 1937. Nov . Print.

Carey, Margaret. "The Forgotten Daughter." *The Times* 2 Feb.
1978, Past Times sec. Print

Mrs. Lizzie Reinhart, Weber. Interview by Leslie L. Haskin. "Mrs.
Lizzie Reinhart Webber." *W.P.A.Project.* 1936?. 1936?. Print.

Mrs. Luella Colbert, Robnett. Interview by Leslie Haskins. *W.P.A.
Works Project.* Approx 1936. Vol 6

Wigle, Mr. Ed. Interview by Leslie L. Haskin. "Mr. Ed Wigle."
W.P.A. Interviews. Approx 1936. Vol. 8

"Past Times" (research by Margaret Carey and Pat Hainline)

"Crook County Genealogical Society Newsletter." April 1, 2007. Accessed August 23, 2014. http://www.bowmanmuseum.org/files/Genealogy.pdf.

Stover, Elsie G. "America Crooks." In *The Pioneer Story*. Prineville: Bend Bulletin, 1950.

Spalding, Eliza. "Speech during the 1894 Linn County Pioneer's Reunion." *The Massacre* (1894). Print.

Certificate of Death for Eliza S. Warren, 21 June 1919, SL No. 26742, State of Idaho Board of Health, Vital Records Section, copy in the possession of author.

McCormick, Linda. "1888." In *Linn County Pioneer Association, Minutes from Meetings from July 30, 1887 to June 18, 1926*, Brownsville, Oregon: Self Published, 2012.

Further Reading:

Paterson, Pamela, Examiner.com, *Tabitha Moffatt Brown (1780 - 1858)*, Sept. 23, 2013 <http://www.examiner.com/article/tabitha-moffatt-brown-1780-1858>

Sevetson, Donald, The Oregon Encyclopedia, *George Atkinson (1819 - 1889)*, Sept. 23, 2013 <http://www.oregonencyclopedia.org/entry/view/atkinson_george_1819_1889_/>

Davis, James W., Idaho Potato commission, *Aristocrat in Burlap, A history of the potato in Idaho*, Chapter 1 Spalding Grows the First Idaho Potatoes, Sept. 23, 2013 <http://www.idahopotato.com/?page=aristocrat_popup&is_popup=1&id=5>

Biography of the author

Linda grew up in Eugene, Oregon, and moved with her family to Southern California where she graduated from high school in Garden Grove. In 1981, she and her husband moved back to the Pacific Northwest and lived in the Portland area. Linda had a long career in the hairdressing business and owned her own salon for many years. The couple retired in Brownsville, Oregon, in 2005. This is where her love of history really blossomed. Linda did historical research for different community events she was involved with, sharpening her research skills. Curiosity about Henry Spalding and his immediate family inspired her to research their story after she found that they lived in Brownsville for a time. The culmination of that data resulted in the journey of writing this book.

Made in the USA
San Bernardino, CA
07 May 2016